To Jerry & Judi
Dear friends of
heart, may peace
blessings always of
your door!
Ginger H.

# k n o w i n g

## *a spiritual memoir of healing and hope*

# knowing

*a spiritual memoir of healing and hope*

**by Ginger Blair**

Website/Blog: www.gingerblair.com

Facebook Page:
www.facebook.com/gingerblair

E-mail: gingerblairauthor@gmail.com

ISBN 978-1-57074-052-7
Printed in the United States of America

Printed By:
Greyden Press, LLC
2251 Arbor Blvd.
Dayton, OH 45439
www.greydenpress.com

# TABLE OF CONTENTS

Acknowledgements vii

Introduction ix

CHAPTER 1

 The Deepest Breath 1

CHAPTER 2

 Empathic Childhood 7

CHAPTER 3

 The Return 23

CHAPTER 4

 Renewal 37

CHAPTER 5

 The Soul's Prescription 49

CHAPTER 6

 The Mirror of Meditation 69

CHAPTER 7

 Transforming Beliefs into Wisdom 95

CHAPTER 8

 Simple Acts 119

CHAPTER 9

 My Validations 169

CHAPTER 10

 Life After Life 199

CHAPTER 11
    Grace through Gratitude      225

Readers Guide      233
About the Author      245

# ACKNOWLEDGMENTS

To my beloved husband, Michael, thank you for your undying belief in me and for giving me the guidance to pursue this effort. I love you...to infinity and beyond.

To my father, Bill Anderson, thank you for allowing me to drink from your well of wisdom and to benefit from your perpetually optimistic thoughts.

To my mother, Penny, who set me on the path to explore beyond religion and opened my world to esoteric wisdom.

To Andy, the best sister a woman could ever wish for, and to her husband, Larry, the brother I never had.

To my family and extended family, you complete my heart.

To my friends and supporters, thank you for believing I could write a book, even when I lacked the knowledge and belief myself.

And to Jennifer Hill Robenalt, Nettie Reynolds, Lynn Kindler, and Jihan Barakah for bringing this book to the public when I had merely envisioned it as a Christmas gift to my family. Your belief in me has been a transforming experience.

May blessings pour down upon all of you who have so blessed my own life.

# INTRODUCTION

How this book you are holding came into being is as much a part of the story as the book itself. For years, people have told me I should write one. My father was one of those people, and I should have taken his advice to heart sooner. He was one of my most welcome advisors in life. Nevertheless, to me, writing a book about my simple life seemed preposterous. I just couldn't see how simplicity and devotion could be interesting to others.

Then one day I went into my office to clean off my desk. Without any conscious forethought whatsoever, my body simply sat down at my computer, and the words you're about to read began to pour forth.

My fingers were on fire, and I could barely keep up with the words that flooded my mind and streamed through my fingertips and onto the pages. It was as though a bottle full of carbonated soda had been shaken and the lid shot off, allowing the contents to spew out like a geyser. I hope these words that flew from my heart then will now flow to yours. As you read, you will see how my life has been guided and directed by a source beyond my own wisdom.

As a cancer survivor of twenty-plus years, my initial purpose for writing about my triumph over cancer was to give hope to others who may be experiencing the same grim prognosis. But as I wrote, I found that I couldn't possibly delve into those experiences without including all the spiritual knowledge I gained through unseen teachers or guides and, most assuredly, from the wisdom we all house within.

One day, while I was immersed in deep meditation, in the midst of my third bout with cancer, I was graced with spontaneous healing. This healing was not only on a physical plane, and it set me on the path that I follow today. It taught me my purpose in life, and it let me know beyond all doubt that we are not alone in this world, that at any given moment, we are being held and guided by the Great Unknown.

From there I realized I had to go back to the very first time I'd had a spiritual encounter, and that's how this book unfolded. These are experiences I've kept mostly to myself or have only shared with those very close to me over the years. In the past I held these stories close to my heart in the belief that sharing them openly and randomly might somehow diminish their significance—that they might lose the extraordinary power they held to continually move me forward on the path like an unseen roadmap.

At that point, my writing took on a broader tone. Not only is my goal to give hope to those suffering from cancer, but also to others who are suffering trauma from any origin; this is the affirmation that there is a way out of turmoil.

My prayer is that something within these pages may strike a chord within you that will set you on a path you need to follow. If, within this book, you find even the smallest spark of light that helps ignite you to find your own connection or strengthen your existing one, then I bow to you. Beyond that, I hope you may be left with the absolute and undeniable belief that we are all cared for and guided, loved and protected, healed and enlightened by the benevolent Invisible One. S/he does exist!

I write this book for those of you who have had cancer or are experiencing some other catastrophic illness. This is for you if you've fallen out of a relationship into which you'd poured your heart and soul. I also write to those of you who may be healthy, happy individuals but feel the call to go more deeply within. Perhaps you're not sure how to do that or you question why you should.

I invite you to substitute your preferred name for God if your preference is different. This name is not meant to be exclusive in any way. Please use the name that resonates with your own heart for the Highest Power that moves in your life. I certainly want to honor and welcome everyone's preference.

The most important thing I want to convey is that I don't share my experiences in any way to exalt myself. Many of you have probably had your own experiences that will help you to relate. I share my spiritual experiences and my healing from cancer to celebrate the Great Unseen, for it is through the grace of the Mystery of all Mysteries that I have these stories to share at all.

Namasté.

# CHAPTER 1

## The Deepest Breath

Stark terror gripped me as I lay there, wrapped in fear under the covers, waiting for it to stop. I didn't realize then that it was a direct answer to the fervent prayers I'd been sending to Heaven, asking for comfort.

I was about nine, and I had just had an argument with my father, my larger-than-life hero. Although it was about some unimportant matter, I was sure that my heart would be broken forever in the wake of our disagreement. In my despair, I felt the only place I could run was to my other Father, the One in Heaven. Sobbing, I prayed, *Please, God, send an angel to me. Please, God, send an angel to me. Please, God, send and angel to me;* I made this plea over and over again without pause.

I waited with great expectation as I repeated those words. I had decided I wouldn't stop asking until my prayer was answered, and somehow I knew that God would not deny me. I so craved comfort that I was unaware of anything as trivial as the passage of time. In the darkness of my bedroom in that late hour, after everyone else went to sleep, it began: this great, all-encompassing, deep breathing in long, drawn-out vibrations, in...out... in...out...in...out.

Deep, heavy, rhythmic breathing came from every corner of the room, loud, long, and slow. I felt the deep breathing penetrating every cell in my body, breathing that came from every particle of air in the room, from every particle of solid matter, from space in the room where there was no space for a breathing entity to fit. It was breathing from above and below me, where I huddled under the covers in suffocating fear.

I was sure my prayers had somehow gone in the wrong direction. I feared they might have been intercepted, and because I didn't understand it, I thought it surely had to be something evil. *Perhaps it's even the devil himself!* I thought. I was so terrified that I ran to my older sister's room, dived under the covers, and spent the final hours of a restless night.

The next day, I didn't mention a word about it, nor did anyone else in my family. I felt I had caused it, so the next morning at breakfast, I waited and watched, but no one else seemed to be aware of it at all.

It happened so many times after that, that I lost count. I eventually noticed that it only happened when I was alone. I finally told my father about it, and he listened intently and without judgment. He promptly began to check the pipes and the heater and various other things that might account for the mysterious sound that a child might interpret as breathing, but none of his attempts resulted in a feasible answer. After his efforts came up empty, I privately came to the conclusion that our house was haunted. Thankfully, we moved a couple years later, when my father was offered better employment in another state.

All went well for a while, and I eventually allowed the experience to settle in the back of my mind. I was sure we'd left "it" behind in our move, until one evening when I was alone in the living room, enjoying a good book. Waiting for my father to come home from work, I was sitting in an upholstered chair when the breathing began again. Loud, slow, drawn-out breaths seemed to come from right behind me, even though the back of the chair was flush with the wall. It then moved out into the room, penetrating all space and every molecule, all the way down to the depths of my soul. In disbelief after the long absence of fear, adrenaline shot through me. The dreaded had returned. Without further thought, my fear propelled me. I jumped up and whirled around and yelled as loudly as I could, "Go away and leave me alone and never come back again!" The breathing obeyed; it immediately stopped, and I never heard it again. Still, it's a memory indelibly and forever etched in my mind, and it wasn't until years later that I found the explanation I sought.

In adulthood, at the beginning of my spiritual searching, I found what is, to me, the most comprehensive explanation of such a phenomenon. A small book, fittingly titled *More Answers*, was dictated (channeled) telepathically through author Maurice

B. Cooke, by the source Hilarion, a name known in theosophical writings. It states:

> We are aware that many will not understand what we mean by Holy Breath, but perhaps we can explain by saying that, at the level from which this dictation is originating, there are inputs of spirituality and light from yet higher planes, in exactly the same way that channels of this kind, scriptures, and way-showers, represent inputs of higher spirituality for your own level. One of the ways in which a higher input comes to this level is in the form of the Holy Breath. There are locations in this particular level where any soul or entity can 'go' in order to be overshadowed by these still higher sources of light and purity. The impulse, which is experienced, comes as a 'breathing,' which we term 'Holy Breath' (the closest English equivalent). A Holy Breath is from the highest possible source. (p. 7)

In Genesis 1, the Bible says, "God used His Breath to create the heavens and the Earth," and "God's Breath" and "Holy Breath" are mentioned several times throughout the Bible. The Holy Spirit is not described anywhere in the Bible as a person; rather, it is instead symbolized by Breath. John 3:8 might easily be interpreted to mean "baptized by the Holy Breath."

I've pondered this mystery for so many years, and on occasion, I still find myself marveling at God's grace in answering my prayers. My only regret is that in my ignorance and fear as a child, I ordered it to "go away and leave me alone and never come back again." In my deeper understanding, although I have invited it back, it has never returned.

I believe this breathing was The Great Comforter who came to me in response to my repetitive plea. I prayed for an angel, and not only did I receive the answer to my prayer, but what came to me that night, according to this explanation, was from the "highest possible source." Even today as I write this, I sit in awe.

I chose to begin this book with this reflection because it was verification for me beyond all doubt that our prayers are heard and they are answered. This knowledge later aided me when I was diagnosed with a catastrophic illness and when I faced and survived an abusive relationship. It has aided me when my heart was broken, and it has aided me through the loss of loved ones. This is my story about illness and recovery, loss and grace, faith and hope, and healing and coming out whole on the other end. The ultimate purpose of this book is to assure you of one thing: IF I CAN DO IT, YOU CAN TOO!

# CHAPTER 2

## Empathic Childhood

I'm sure I provided my family with a great source of entertainment in childhood when I shared some of my beliefs and experiences. Although they never laughed at me and, in fact, treated my theories with the utmost respect, I eventually felt it was best to keep most of these things to myself, since no one else seemed to have similar experiences to talk about. Wanting desperately not to call attention to myself, my keen sense of the unspoken indicated it was better to fit in rather than to appear different. We were a close-knit family of four: my sister, my mother, my father, and me.

We were also a family of opposites. My mother was an outgoing adventurer, my father a laidback optimist, and while I was quiet and shy, my sister was the life of the party. I grew up observing her, learning from her actions what worked and what didn't work with my parents. I witnessed the praise heaped upon her when she made choices that worked and the repercussions when they didn't, and I learned a lot from those moments. From watching and learning from her examples, my life went much more smoothly. You might say she paved my way.

As my parents were great lovers of the outdoors, we often spent time in nature. They loved to fish in the clear mountain waters, and while my sister would read, I'd explore. Sometimes I'd climb up and sit for long periods, in the high branches of tall trees until my parents called me back to Earth. I suppose I was a strange child. Sitting around the campfire at night, my father would scare the bejesus out of us with his ghost stories. My sister and I would cover our heads and grab each other in fright, then beg him not to stop. Living with my parents was always an adventure.

Those were idyllic times in our lives, a nostalgic period we'd often refer back to for years to come, always with great fondness. Still, as beautiful as those memories were, those experiences weren't enough to sustain my parents' marriage. They were simply cut from different fabric.

It was during my summer break, between third and fourth grade, when our family of four broke apart. My father was devastated at the thought of the divorce, and I remained fiercely loyal to him. His first single residence was a tiny upstairs apartment that overlooked the main street in town. I spent long afternoons tracing picture after picture from Walt Disney coloring books, then filling in the lines with color; Bambi was my favorite. Each picture went to my father, who would carefully pin them up on his bare walls. My heart ached for us all in our separation. Years later, my father told me when he was at his lowest point during that time, he had contemplated taking his own life. He said looking at those pictures I'd colored made him realize suicide was not an option, and that admission had a profound effect on me.

When my little friends offered consolation because my parents didn't live together anymore, I'd always rush to reassure them, saying something like, "But it's okay. My parents still *really* like each other." Of course I was in denial, masking my own pain, but it seemed true to me at the time.

As time healed their wounds, the fondness that remained between my parents began to reemerge. They eventually became more like brother and sister than exes, and I noticed this new relationship served us all very well. With the pressure off their differences that were magnified under one roof, all those unkind words between them receded. Living in a small town, visitation was flexible, and soon we settled into a new family arrangement.

Organized religion had never been a large part of our lives, not before or after the divorce, though we did go to church on what we termed special occasions, but that did not include every week. My sister and I were essentially left to our own devices when it came to religion. This is not to say we didn't discuss God; we did, for how could our family enjoy nature so much without wondering how such grandeur was created? It was just a very relaxed teaching, and our mother and father didn't try to force us to conform to any one church. My mother was always esoteric in her beliefs, and I'm grateful to her for showing me a different way to look at life and religion.

Extended family members were Mormon, Catholic, or Baptist, so we would have had a whole menu from which to choose if we had been so inclined. Besides the moral conduct my parents instilled in us, the occasional talk about divinity, and the many astronomy lessons my father taught me in our back yard at night or camping under the stars, I allowed nature to serve as my church.

Through my experiences with nature, I always felt connected to some Higher Power. I grew up feeling I had *two* fathers: one I could give big hugs to at night before sleep and the great Other, with whom I could share my innermost secrets and never feel misunderstood. In essence, nature is God manifested, so I have never felt completely alone, not even when no one else has been with me. Years later, I was present when Dan Rather, award-winning reporter and news anchor, spoke. He was a man who'd been in life-threatening assignments more than once. The lasting thing I took away from his interview was his comment about faith: "If you have faith, you are never alone." Those words penetrated me to my core and completely captured how I've felt my whole life. Though I didn't go to church every Sunday, unseen sources strengthened my faith, led me, and guided my spiritual education.

When I was a young child, my father worked for the Atomic Energy Commission (AEC), while the government was testing atomic bombs in southern Utah. He was tasked with mapping out and building roads into these remote areas for research. Often and quite literally, we lived out in the middle of nowhere in base-camp communities. Mobile homes and temporary housing arrangements aside, my mother often told us my father's days with the AEC were some of her happiest memories.

While in these remote areas, we'd travel into town once or twice a week for supplies and to visit my sister. She was five years older and lived in town with relatives to attend school while I stayed with our parents. We had never been apart before and I missed her terribly.

In her absence, my playmates were my invisible friends, whom I visited daily under a large Juniper tree. Since I was so small in size, to me, it felt like a majestic, safe harbor. I would crawl under its huge canopy of drooping limbs, where I could remain completely hidden from the outside world. There was plenty of room to spare when I nestled up close to the trunk, and the floor of my "living room" was carpeted in soft needles so the smell was clean and pure. It was a perfect playhouse.

I'd sit there with my invisible friends, who were quite real to me because I was given more and more information to confirm beyond any doubt what some called my "wacky" belief system. Their teachings were transmitted to me as "knowing." There were no audible words spoken between us; rather, the teachings were communicated as blocks of information placed deeply inside me. Like an ice cube melts in the sun, the information would melt into me as I assimilated it through my entire being. No questions were asked. The transmissions I received were always crystal clear and complete, with an undeniable purity of truth. In my spiritual education through the Unseen, I learned at an early age that there is life in all things. I learned that the Earth is a living, breathing organism, that each time a bomb was set off, it not only damaged the skin of the Earth, but it also damaged the air, the water, and ultimately the health of those who lived downwind of the incredible fallout that resulted from such detonations during the testing. These were the things my unseen friends taught me long before the damage became common knowledge.

The government defended its actions to the end, declaring, "All precautions were taken!" and "Nothing will be harmed because we're testing only in remote locations." But I knew better. I knew the information given to me under that Juniper tree was correct when my grandmother, whose ranch was downwind of those test sites, died of leukemia.

Years later, too far into the future to benefit my grandmother, a class action lawsuit was settled between the government and the many residents, who, like my grandmother, had been diagnosed with leukemia and a host of other health issues. Not only had our beautiful Earth been ravaged, but its population was suffering as a result. I was too young for school at the time, but I knew in the core of my being that mankind was violating the laws of the universe. I knew because I'd been taught by my invisible friends, under the Juniper tree.

Today, I don't automatically discount as imaginary the invisible friends with whom a child converses, for it was under the Juniper tree that the wise ones taught me the truer meaning of knowing right from wrong.

When I was no more than four or five years old, my mother found me going through our kitchen garbage bin one day. Of course she wanted to know what I was doing. I remember explaining that I was looking for another soup can to go with the one I was holding so it wouldn't be lonely. My mother assured me that soup cans have no life in them but somewhere deep, deep inside, I felt she was wrong.

Scientists have now confirmed that all particles in the universe have a vibratory quality, a life all their own. Even a rock, when hooked up to a seismograph, vibrates at a very low level. Without awareness of this scientific data at that time, today I realize that this is what I call the "knowing" behind my actions.

To me, there were simply different versions of life, whether it was in the vibratory frequency of a rock, a lonely soup can, or a human being. Energy vibrates within all things, albeit at a different rate in each thing. I don't know how I sensed this. My intent with the soup cans had been to place them side by side as they waited for disposal. In my childlike mind, that would prevent either from being alone. I was sure they could resonate together until they became what I termed friends. Today, scientific data supports at least part of my childhood theory. Perhaps my caring nature carried it a bit too far when I pictured two empty cans enjoying the experience of friendship, but "resonating together" is a perfect way to convey this. It's further explained by scientific research on entrainment, which I will talk about later.

> *" In the one perception of God's universal love... stones, trees, water, earth, all things will embrace you and welcome you to their one heart-altar of light."*
> **Paramahansa Yogananda**

It was incredibly painful for me when I reached school age and we moved back to the city so I could begin kindergarten. I sensed that life as I knew it, was being deserted, completely left behind, and I was not looking forward to that new stage of my development. I remember riding to school on the very first day, engulfed by dread and depression. My sister and her best friend had opted for the window seats, and I sat in the middle, staring into the back of the front seat, too small to see out of any of the windows. I remember begrudgingly realizing that I still had *years* ahead of me before that routine would end. It was agony to think of giving up the freedom of my education in nature for the four walls of a classroom, but I kept those feelings inside. Throughout my childhood, I had the feeling somewhere inside that I was waiting, even though I never knew *what* I was waiting for. Sometimes I was overcome with the grim sense that my whole lifetime would just be one more long exercise I had to get through.

As I was growing up, adults would continually comment on

how mature I was for my age, perhaps because I was so serious much of the time or because I really was unexpectedly mature. In retrospect, the common thread that ran through my earlier life was that when I spoke, adults paid close attention to what I had to say. Sometimes I was described as "wise beyond her age." I learned to accept their appraisal and that, perhaps, reinforced my seriousness. It wasn't until I was seventeen that the thought struck me: *I've been mature all my life! Did I miss my childhood?* I realized if I were ever to enjoy being an adolescent, I'd better do it then, before others *expected* me to act maturely. I put great effort into acting like a kid, but it was no use; seriousness and good sense were threads in the very fabric of my being. As I grew older, however, I was able to lighten up and find great joy in life.

I'm sure many of you who are reading this can relate, but my level of sensitivity and compassion has created a lot of pain for me. It doesn't matter whether an injustice is committed against a human, plant, or animal; if I am near, I *feel* it. My childhood was before the metaphysical movement and the growing consensus of the Oneness of all creation.

In fact, I have only recently learned that I'm an empath. It was a huge relief to put a name to it, to find out that there are others out there like me. Most of my life, I've wondered why I was different, thinking I was the only one in the world whose eyes would fill with tears at the least provocation. Most empaths experience a deep sense of knowing and sensitivity around others, even among plants and animals, and this stirs up intense feelings. I was always told that I was extremely sensitive, but I could never describe the depth of my emotions.

Empaths not only deal with the five senses, but we also experience patterns of vibration emanating from outside ourselves. The vibratory emotions of others instantly mirror themselves within us. In essence, we're able to eavesdrop on the feelings of others, as though their emotions were our own.

Like many empaths, I'm somehow able to experience subtle changes in other people, animals, and even objects based on my interactions with them or when I'm in close proximity to them. We don't even have to know others to pick up on this vibratory field. I'm often embarrassed when I feel another person's strong emotions, such as despair or pain, and inadvertently become emotionally moved. Due to the depth of the feelings perceived and the empathy they evoke, I may tear up in public when there seems to be no explanation for my watery eyes and red nose. It can be an awkward situation, especially if I'm among those who don't know me well. Luckily, most of my friends and my husband have come to accept me for who and how I am, and we make light of it.

The flipside of this sensitivity is that it serves me well when I give counsel. I begin from a place of understanding, through feeling what the other person is experiencing rather than having to determine the issue through words and explanations.

On two different occasions, once in a crowded restaurant and once in a grocery store, I so acutely felt the pain of a stranger that I asked if I could help in any way, even though not a word had yet passed between us. I half-expected to be brushed off; however, these people greatly needed a release, and we found a quiet corner in which to talk. It was extraordinary to hold their hearts in mine as they shared their stories with me as if I were a trusted confidante, though we had met only moments before.

Another time, I gained new employment in a place where I had wanted to work for some time. Everyone was busy but friendly, and after a short while, I grew to love the work and the atmosphere. One of my co-workers was especially intriguing, quiet but always very pleasant. Though I liked her a lot, I didn't know her well at all. Nevertheless, I couldn't shake the deep sadness that enveloped me each time I was near her, even when she was at the end of a long hallway, removed from my area. Eventually, after I got to know everyone better, I asked about her. I was told she had lost her three children when her home had burned down eight years before.

As a child, my empathy toward animals was particularly deep. Next to nature, they were my solace. Energy flowed between us as we merged into one through my process of bonding with the senses. Their pain was my pain; their fear my fear; and their sense of contentment or hunger became my own when I went into this state of communion. This was another of my peculiarities that I never mentioned to others while growing up. I just assumed feelings of that sort were experienced by all, although I did notice that no one else seemed to be as deeply affected as I was when an animal was in distress.

When I was very small, I reacted to what I clearly thought was an injustice to an animal. Exasperated, my mother knelt beside me as I sat on the kitchen floor in a puddle of tears. With her arms around me, she asked me, "Why do you love animals *so* much?" To this day, I remember my clear and ready response. I looked deeply into her eyes and answered, "Because animals won't hurt us." Of course I was speaking in psychological terms, not in terms of meat-eating creatures or rabid beasts. I don't remember what emotional wound I may have suffered to give me that knowledge, as I was only four or five at the time, but the knowledge was deep within me. I knew beyond a shadow of a doubt that animals don't play with our feelings.

The ability to detect life current is also a mystery. Whether it's in an animal or a browned and broken plant, I somehow sense whether a life force still burns within. This also holds true for "dead" animals alongside the road. Even though the unconscious animal may appear to be dead, a life force may still glow within.

On more than one occasion, I was able to convince my understanding parents to turn our speeding car around to render aid. We didn't stop at every animal along the way, of course, as some were wild, and my parents didn't know what we'd do with them if they did manage to survive. Others were less fortunate, and the flicker of life no longer burned in them. But whenever I convinced my parents to stop, there was always the presence of living energy in each body we saved. Somehow I detected that vibration, even passing by at sixty-five miles an hour.

One particularly vivid memory involving animals has stayed with me. I'm not sure how old I was, but I was young enough that my parents wouldn't yet leave me at home alone. Since no one else was available to keep tabs on me during their absence, I had no choice but to join them on a hunting trip during deer season. Dread buried me. Several family members, my mother included, were along for the hunt.

My brother-in-law was the brother I never had, so I chose to accompany him after we reached the destination; for some reason, I felt safest with him. Each of the hunters chose their own way as we trekked over hill after hill, and he kept his gun ready. Eventually he motioned to me with a finger to his lips and pointed across the vastness to a small dot on a faraway hill. Unable to tear my eyes away from the target, I watched it disappear when the shot pierced the dense silence.

In my heart, I knew that although the deer was down, there was still life energy coursing through its body, and I shared that fact with my brother-in-law. "No, it was a clean shot," he assured me. "You don't need to worry." Still, I insisted; not only was it alive and wounded, I felt it was not a full-grown deer at all. To calm my worries, he assured me the distance made it look small.

We continued to argue back and forth as we walked over one hill, then another, in the direction of the felled deer. I was in anguish. I had seen only a small speck in the distance, but I was connected to the animal's energy as much as if we had one beating heart. My brother-in-law repeatedly assured me but when we finally arrived, before us lay a small, young, mortally wounded deer. Not wanting it to suffer any more than it had, he put it out of its misery.

Evidently the look on my face said it all, for my brother-in-law told me several years later that on that day, he began to lose his taste for the "sport."

## FAITH

In elementary school, I didn't know about faith, per se. I only knew that if I trusted the Heavenly Presence enough, I would get what S/He wanted to give me. My belief was unshakeable, even though at that age, I had no clue of the definition of *faith*.

In sixth grade, my trust was solidified. It was Christmas, and our classroom had been decorated for the holiday. A large poster depicting Mary had been drawn in colored chalk and hung at the front of the classroom, and I thought it was incredibly beautiful.

The time came to remove the holiday decorations before school adjourned for Christmas break, and the teacher asked if anyone would like to have the poster. My hand shot up, along with several others'. To decide who would take the poster home, we wrote our names on pieces of paper and placed them in a bowl for a drawing, but that didn't really matter. I already knew with dead certainty that the poster was meant to go home with me.

Realizing I needed a plan to make my piece of paper stand out from the others, I thought long and hard, all the while feeling God would handle it for me. I wrote my name in large, printed letters and folded it six or seven times, until it resembled a small wad; the others were conformed into flat folded sheets that would lie limply in the bottom of the bowl. After placing mine in the bowl that was then raised above our heads, I waited as the teacher's hand extended through the air and dipped inside to bring me victory.

Did my name get chosen because I had made my paper larger than the others, or was it because my faith had been supported in the unseen realm? My answer would be a resounding, "Both!" Who do you think gave me the idea to make my paper stand out from the others?

I bow in deep gratitude whenever I realize there is more at play in our lives than mere coincidence. It was Sigmund Freud who coined the phrase, "There are no coincidences," and I believe that to be true.

We may continue to chalk up everything that comes to us as mere coincidence, but in reality, with each occurrence, we're being given the opportunity to look deeper and delve into the mystery behind each unfolding experience. The Universe constantly beckons us toward a deeper connection.

Around the time I took the poster home, I secretly decided I wanted to be a nun. Though I didn't know anything about the Catholic faith or the rigors of becoming a nun, I had a Catholic friend who invited me to attend Sunday Mass with her one Sunday. I had never seen such opulence. It seemed the whole interior of the church was gold. I decided right then and there that becoming a nun was surely the deepest way I could show my love to God. Giving up everything in the outside world seemed a small price to pay, at the time when I was a small child in a small world.

I was about twelve when my hormones kicked in, and my interior life began to recede into the background. As life often does, it had other plans for me, and I never pursued that goal, but it was through that collection of childhood experiences that my feet became firmly planted in God's garden.

*"Intellectually I touched God many times as truth, and emotionally, I touched God as love. I touched God as goodness. I touched God as kindness. It came to me that God is a creative force, a motivating power, an overall intelligence, an ever-present, all-pervading spirit which binds everything in the universe together and gives life to everything. That brought God close. I could not be where God is not. You are God. God is within you."*
***Peace Pilgrim***

# CHAPTER 3

## The Return

Fast forward now, through teen years and education, through boyfriends, employment opportunities, and a bad marriage. These are the years where many of us get so caught up in our everyday lives and our accomplishments that we often lose sight of the underlying purpose of why we are here in the first place. I'm no exception.

When things are going our way, we feel on top of the world. We often feel *we* are the doers, that our efforts alone are the sole reason for the success we are enjoying  As we enjoy the fruits of our labor, we can be deluded and get farther and farther from the truth. Often it takes a hard bump in the road to jolt us, to force us to seek something higher, or to find something to fill the void after the world has deemed us successful. That bump can be the emptiness of a broken relationship, lost job opportunities, loss of direction after a major goal has been achieved, or, worse, health concerns may arise.

These traumatic events get our attention. They can serve as

catalysts bringing us back to our knees in order that we may give our attention to God. Sometimes these setbacks are needed to take us back to center and awaken our true sense of our original purpose. Many of us pray when things get rough, but we need to remember to also do so when times are good.

Without these bumps in the road to awaken us, weariness can set in, or a dis-ease with our lives comes to the foreground. When this occurs, either we continue to simply put one foot in front of the other year after year, with our shoulders hunched and our gaze turned downward until we become so dulled that our original radiance becomes a dim glow, or else we seek change.

My first marriage was a relatively short one. I had known my ex-husband for a few years before I married him. He worked in the movie industry, and he bumped shoulders with many celebrities and movie stars. It all seemed very intriguing to me.

He was married at the time, and he and his wife made a nice couple, though their marriage didn't endure. After they divorced, he periodically dropped into the office where I worked to visit a colleague. They were close friends.

Whenever he stopped in, we always exchanged greetings and short conversations. We married less than a year after we started dating; though it seemed way too fast to me, but I didn't listen to my guidance. You know, guidance is that nudge that tries to get our attention so we can think about things before we act. I simply pushed that recurring feeling aside and blindly plunged ahead.

It wasn't until we'd been together several months that I began to notice that all was not as I thought it to be. Over time, I began to realize that I really didn't know the person I had committed to share my life with. I also began to suspect that he had a drinking problem.

I always had a hard time convincing him to go to the movies with me. He'd inevitably complain that he worked in the movie business and didn't want to sit through them in his free time as well. I would occasionally insist, as I missed going to the movies, but whenever we did go to the cinema or theater, I discovered that hiding beers in my purse was a requirement; apparently, two hours without a drink wasn't an option.

Things only worsened when I discovered alcohol was not his only drug of choice. There were swings between Mr. Erratic and Mr. Nice, but before I knew it, Mr. Erratic became the norm. We had a very unsavory, short marriage, and I was lost at the thought of the mistake I'd made. I'd always been the one everyone came to for counsel, and there I was, at the bottom of the heap myself. I couldn't shake the thought so many of us ask ourselves so often in life: *How could this happen to me?* To top it off, toward the end of our marriage, I was diagnosed with cancer for the third time in ten years.

When I was diagnosed the first time in my early thirties, I

heard somewhere that the diagnosis often arose about eighteen months to three years after a traumatic event. I'm not sure how true that is for others, but it definitely fit my experience. My fiancé of eight years had been killed in an accident just three years prior.

I went into my doctor's office on a Thursday, only to be told that I was scheduled for a complete hysterectomy four days later. In shock, I remember asking something like: "But isn't that Step Ten on a one-to-ten scale? Aren't there other options before we do *that*?"

When we were small, people often asked my sister and me, "What do you want to be when you grow up?" My sister consistently answered, "I want to be a mother," but I always said, "I want to travel." Up until that moment in that doctor's office, as I took in the grim news, I had never considered children of my own. It wasn't that I didn't like children; I just hadn't ever been with anyone I could see myself continuing to be with for the rest of my life. The one thing I knew for sure was that I didn't want to raise a child alone.

Though I had usually been content in my partnerships, my intuition always seemed to look farther ahead, and I could see those relationships ending one day. I could sense, even when I was most happy, that a discontinuance would eventually occur somewhere down the road. I somehow sensed all my relationships as being merely for now instead of forever.

Perhaps I manifested those endings, or perhaps it was my sixth sense, my guidance, that gave me the wisdom to know that children weren't a part of those plans. But there, in that doctor's office, I was being told that my physical ability to have children was about to be extinguished out of necessity, to preserve my life. My response surprised me. I hadn't realized the importance of choice in the matter until then, as I'd always felt in control of it.

After much arguing with my doctor, we opted for interim steps instead of going for the whole enchilada. Two years later, however, I was diagnosed again. I underwent conventional Western medical treatments two of the three times when cancerous cells appeared in my cervix. When it returned for the third time, a deep certainty guided me to try alternative methods of healing.

The things I knew were few: My relationship was so out of balance that it had to reflect back on the health of my body; my employment in a negative environment was not serving my best interests anymore, regardless of the fact that the salary was exceptionally good; and my connection with God was begging for my attention, after having been placed on the back-burner in my life.

As I matured I had gotten drawn into the outer world of distraction, and my invisible friends had grown quiet. I had been so busy supposedly "living" life that I hadn't even noticed. Now, loneliness engulfed me, and I craved the guidance and communication, the togetherness and meaning they had provided from the time I was born. Father Thomas Keating captured the essence of my loneliness in *Open Mind, Open Heart* when he wrote: "The Divine presence has always been with us, but we think it absent. That thought is the monumental illusion of the human condition. The spiritual journey is to heal it."

After the great relief, when the breathing ceased to haunt me, I was swept into daily activities and unconsciously moved matters of God farther and farther to the back of my mind. I was busy having it all and had no time for questioning my purpose. As I perceived it, my purpose was to finish my education, to gain employment, and to find a lasting relationship. I lived over a thousand miles away from the people who had guided me in my younger years, and I thought being on my own was what I had been waiting for. I began to realize throughout the illness that what I'd really been waiting for my whole life was my reunion with the Divine. More importantly, I had been furnished enough information from my invisible friends in childhood to know that I didn't have to die to achieve it!

In his book, *Going Home,* Tich Nhat Hanh identifies our cultural wounds and delves into ways to heal them. The wound he says he sees most often is our "alienation from our own spiritual traditions." I knew nothing about meditation or alternative healing. Neither did I have any contrived plan or direction, except to know that I had to quit my job that was steeped in negativity; end my marriage to an alcoholic husband; and heed my guidance in order to heal one final time.

During that time of personal revelation, while I was standing at the receptionist's desk in my dentist's office, she looked at my hands and asked me if I was practicing Jin Shin Jyutsu. Confused by her question, I looked down to where she was looking. My hands were together in front of my body, with one hand holding the index finger of the opposite one.

I'm sure my face registered a huge question mark, as I didn't have the slightest clue what she meant. She seemed embarrassed about asking and quickly went back to work, but before I left, I found her again and questioned her about her comment. She shyly explained that she knew a woman who did energy work, and the odd position I'd been holding my hands in was one of the energy flows found in that healing technique. This is further proof that our bodies know what we need in order to heal, even if we are unaware on a conscious level. My hands had naturally positioned themselves in a healing posture, a healing posture in a modality with which I was not yet familiar. Needless to say, I asked for the name and number of the energy worker. It was there, in that dentist's office that I began following the signs given to me on my healing quest.

Jin Shin Jyutsu, as I later learned, is an ancient oriental healing Art that predates Buddha and Moses; wherein life energy in the body is harmonized, or returned to a state of balance. Literally translated, it is the Art of the Creator expressed through knowing and compassionate man.

When I first met the energy worker, I didn't know what to expect. I had never had so much as a massage, much less anything like what the receptionist had told me about. Little did I know, but it would be the beginning of a long and lasting friendship.

She was a tall, slender, pleasant woman, and her house smelled like sandalwood incense. To brief me before we began, she explained that Jin Shin Jyutsu opens up the meridian flows and frees up the energy inside our bodies. When the blocked energy is freed, the body regains its natural rhythm, its balance, and healing can occur from within.

She instructed me to lie on a padded table, fully clothed, and she moved both of her hands from this place to that, seemingly taking readings from each area she touched. She held her hands in various positions using minimal pressure; the right on one area and the left on another. It reminded me of a fine, elegant dance, except that her feet remained still. I felt a deep stillness and calm envelop me.

After we had finished our first session, I continued to see her periodically, and I could definitely feel the power in her work. My confusion turned to clarity, and aimless wandering birthed direction as my energy channels opened and released the life force within me. I knew then that I was finally on the right path.

Soon after these sessions ended, I felt drawn to go to Santa Fe on what I like to call a healing quest. There are so many alternative healing modalities practiced there that I was sure it would be the perfect place for me. I felt I'd be guided to the next steps, and that I'd recognize those steps when they presented themselves. I was completely filled with trust.

I wandered the streets of Santa Fe, exploring on foot to increase my exercise and conserve my cash, since I was no longer employed. Walking also allowed me to learn the city and see all that it had to offer. Based on my solo adventures during that time of exploration and discovery, Santa Fe continues to be one of my favorite destinations yet today.

As I was walking one day, I was startled by the words "asparagus root." The words had been spoken in a man's voice, and though I didn't hear them through my ears, they were received nonetheless, as though they'd been telepathically transmitted.

Beyond being surprised, I was confused as well, especially since I'd never heard of anything called asparagus root. The words came periodically to mind as I continued to walk by the quaint little shops that line the city streets; anyone who has had the pleasure of visiting Santa Fe will know exactly what I mean. "Asparagus root...asparagus root...asparagus root..." The tempo of the words as they circulated through me gradually quickened.

I stepped off the curb and crossed the street at a random location, only to end up in front of a curious little shop sitting at an angle to the corner. It had a flat front that sat catty-corner to the sharp corner where the streets intersected. It gave the store a unique appearance from the others, whose sharp side corners matched the corners of the side streets. The front of the building was glass, and the wood and glass doors were propped open wide, beckoning me to enter.

The sun was setting behind the building, and they had not yet turned on the lights. As the interior was somewhat dark, I took a few slow steps inside to give my eyes time to adjust after being out in the sunny streets. There, in front of me on a countertop, were intriguing glass containers that looked like tall, clear cookie jars. The contents of the jars varied, but the one that caught my attention the most had twig-like sticks poking out of the top. As I read the label I froze; those crooked, printed letters taped on the front of the jar spelled "Asparagus root." Without knowing it, I had stumbled into a Chinese herb shop.

There, I learned that in traditional Chinese medicine, asparagus root is used for a long litany of ailments, including cancer. For the duration of my stay in Santa Fe, I walked around town chewing those roots as if my life depended on it.

After I learned the city streets and culture from the inside out, my intuition grew stronger. I knew my healing process had to come from within me, not from any outside source. I realized I didn't need to go away to accomplish this task - it could be done in the sanctuary of my own home. As much as I enjoyed my time in Santa Fe, I realized those explorations simply diverted my thoughts from my problems, but in the process, they had brought a return to balance and much-needed quietude after my tumultuous marriage and the scary health news. My stamina had returned with slow-paced exercise. Balance had taken root in me through the simple process of walking and listening and trusting.

I caught a flight to return to Texas and my new residence. I knew it was time to turn inward, and I had the perfect setting in which to do so. My neighborhood was new to me, so neighbors would no longer drop by unexpectedly; for in my new environment, I knew no one.

My friends all assumed I'd be in Santa Fe all summer, seeking alternative healing, so I wasn't included in any of their plans. My setting was new and fresh and didn't carry the vibrations of trauma that my previous home would have harbored. But best of all it was *quiet*, and I knew it would remain so.

I began to meditate in the peace and quiet of my surroundings, for only five minutes at first, albeit several times a day. Not having a clue how to begin, I just followed my inner guidance. I had never read any books on meditation, but with deep intention and patience, the more I practiced, the deeper I was able to go. I was an eager student, and my desire to connect with the Silent Source burned inside me. I trusted that I'd be shown the way, and my patience eventually paid off.

When I began, I didn't even know enough about the spiritual path to know what to read, so I called my friend, the energy worker, to ask for some recommendations. She suggested four books to get me started and directed me to a nearby metaphysical bookstore. The first book on the list just didn't call to me, but I bought the second book on the list. Then I bought the third book on the list and devoured it. Finally, I bought the fourth and final book, and I still didn't feel called or compelled to read the book that was first on the list. In fact, I didn't read that first book until a few years later.

Each spare moment was spent either in meditation or reading the spiritual books I had found. When I finished three of the four books, I didn't have a clue what to do next. The books were like stepping stones; though they pointed me in the right direction, they didn't get me to the destination.

I was in agony, feeling I had hit the proverbial wall, and I had no idea how to propel myself forward. The only idea that came to me was to fall on my knees and cry out to the Heavens for help. Although I'm not Catholic, I probably would have joined a convent at that point had there been one in the neighborhood, so burning was my desire for guidance and connection.

My heart called out so fervently, so desperately for God and His comfort that He absolutely could not deny me, and He responded. Sometimes, my awareness of His presence was preceded by a deep *hum*, like energy going through an electrical wire. Sometimes there was no sound at all, but the comfort and love that enveloped me cannot be explained in language alone. The Great Quiet was exactly that—a quiet so deep that I was aware of nothing other than the knowledge that I was not alone, that I was loved beyond measure. I needed nothing else.

Each time I sat, I filled my heart to the brim with love for the Quiet Listener, and He continued to accept my invitations. The more He answered, the longer and more often I wanted to sit, until we did that dance together for about six weeks, without outside intrusion. Only an occasional trip to the grocery store or bookstore interrupted us.

In the Bible, the number forty is mentioned on numerous occasions. Moses wandered in the desert for forty years; Noah built his ark to save them from The Great Flood, when it rained for forty days and forty nights; and so on. These stories refer to purification, just as mine does. My blessed retreat and healing experience had lasted about six weeks, approximately forty days, and it was the most incredible experience of my life!

*"Faith is not belief without proof but*
*trust without reservation."*
*Patrick Overton*

# CHAPTER 4

## Renewal

Allow me to interject that the following is not to be taken as medical advice, for I am not a doctor of any sort. Here, I'm simply relating my own personal experience. We must each find our own way, as everyone has their remedies, whether those cures are found through holistic methods or traditional medicine. Much of healing involves trial and error, and doctors do not recommend a one-size-fits-all approach for those who are ill. Thus, I urge you to find your own connection with Source or within the medical community to find the instruction that fits your own individual needs. Healing is something like a safe: There is only one combination that will open it, and the combination that worked for me was tailor-made for me in the state I was in at that particular moment, mentally, emotionally, physically, and spiritually. We must each find our own path, whether through illness or good health. One of my teachers from India put it more eloquently:

*"Everything in creation has individuality. The Lord never repeats Himself. Similarly, in man's divine search there are infinite variations of approach and expression. The romance of each devotee with God is unique."*
*Paramahansa Yogananda*

My instructions were clear from the beginning. Through my deep yearning, I had connected sufficiently to The Divine Physician, The Greatest Doctor of All Time. I received specific, timely guidance, right down to my diet, and I didn't question any of it. I simply followed that prescription, knowing that wherever it was taking me had to be a better place than where I'd been.

By listening to my body, I was guided to eat nothing but cool, refreshing watermelon. It was easy enough to do so, since my body didn't *want* anything other than watermelon. It helped that we were going into one of the hottest summers on record. It was May in Texas, and temperatures had already started to climb. My next instruction was to add raw almonds to my diet. Eventually, toward the end of my divinely inspired menu, a few other healthful foods were added as well.

I knew nothing of nutrition at the time, and I didn't realize until years later that I was undergoing a purification process. I now know that watermelon is full of nutrition. Of all the fruits and vegetables, it is the highest source of lycopene, a powerful antioxidant that helps us fight several types of cancer and heart disease, just to name a couple of its health benefits. Watermelon is also full of water, of course, and that helped to flush debris from my system, washing me clean. The natural sugar in the melon gave me energy while I was going through the detoxification process. When the almonds were added, those provided my body with protein, calcium, and a myriad of phytochemicals that are also thought to protect against cancer, though I didn't know that at the time. My physical activity was greatly reduced because I spent so much time reading or meditating or learning from the spiritual lectures I rented. The sugar and water from the watermelon and the drinking from the Divine in meditation kept me well hydrated, physically and spiritually.

Sometimes our greatest spiritual growth comes about when we have no knowledge at all, when we can go beyond any preconceived ideas or notions of how or when something should happen. At that time, my mind was a clear slate. I just took it as it came, day by day, in the bliss of reunion. I didn't have a clue what to expect, so consequently, I expected nothing. Rather, I just allowed myself to follow the next step as it was revealed to me.

Through my knowing, I was instructed to continue the daily two-mile walks I had begun in Santa Fe. I didn't try to qualify any of the instructions that came to me; I was an open vessel of trust. Those walks through my tree-lined neighborhood were the only times, other than the grocery store and an occasional trip to the bookstore, when I left my home. As I walked, I filled my lungs with fresh air, and my skin drank in the sunlight.

The instructions continued: Read only spiritual writings or watch spiritual programs; walk two miles each day and get two hours of sun; no television, no outside distractions, no friendly lunches or gatherings; no work; and no relationships other than the one shared with Him.

Dust began to accumulate on all of my tabletops, and I let it. What a test that could have been for me, but somehow I innately sensed what was truly important and what wasn't. My previous habit had been to keep everything spotless. Later, when I studied lessons from Self-Realization Fellowship, I learned that habits are detrimental obstacles to our spiritual growth. My guidance had led me to break the habit of obsessive cleaning. I later learned that compulsivity such as cleaning obsessions, eating disorders, shopping addictions, and the like all share a common theme: Those who practice these are trying to find one small area in their lives to exert control, to soothe fear and frustration over our feelings of lack of control or powerlessness. I had certainly felt powerless in my previous marriage, but when we connect with the perfect souls we are, our compulsions dissolve.

A wonderful metaphysical bookstore was in close proximity, and I eagerly rented lectures of famous self-help gurus, motivational speakers, masters of positive thinking, spiritual programs, and documentaries about famous saints. You name it, I read and watched it, all the while yearning for a connection with a higher Source.

Though I now know that staying in silence greatly enhances spiritual progress, I didn't know this at the time. In spite of my conscious unawareness of it, my knowing and guidance kept my vocalization to a minimum, except for the necessary conversations I had at the bookstore or grocery and except for the loving words I shared with Herbie and Betty Jo, my two cat companions.

Other than those times, and a weekly call to my family, meditation was the only form of communication I desired.

My sleepless nights turned into peaceful rest. Meditating as much as I was, I found that I needed much less sleep than before. If I awoke from sleep at any hour of the night because my body was rested, I would go into my meditation room and meditate or read. The clock didn't matter. There was only God's schedule, and if I became tired the next day from awakening in the night, I would simply rest. I didn't need to be anyplace at any given time, and no schedule existed except for the one Spirit was creating spontaneously for me.

Creativity exploded within me. One night, I awoke from a deep sleep and literally threw back the covers on my bed and dashed into my office to capture the words that were pouring through me. I was like a fountain that had been suddenly turned on.

Through the combination of healthful eating, daily sun and fresh air, exercise, rest and meditation, virtual silence, and keeping myself in a cocoon of positive living, balance had returned to my body, as well as to my psyche.

As I was coming out of meditation one day, I was what I can only describe as "swept away." It was as though I had traveled to a different realm. I found myself carried along in what felt like a great, waterless river. I was swept up in some sort of flow that was infused with living energy and consciousness. I was as small as the smallest particle, yet I was part of every single thing in creation—not just every living thing as we know it, but in *everything*. Simultaneously with the smallness, I felt larger than the Universe. I was the space in between, comprising all things. I was the vastness of the Universe and beyond, yet at the same time, I was the space in and around each vibrating molecule.

I was traveling at a great speed in what seemed like a living flow. In fact, I was traveling so fast that I can only compare it to the speed of light. I remember experiencing a state of wonder. I wasn't thinking; I was simply experiencing, traveling in a pure state of joy, like a wide-eyed astronaut on her first trip through space. But then it happened. My mind kicked in, and I distinctly remember thinking, *How can I be traveling so fast without my hair blowing?* I *am* a woman, after all.

Instantly, I was back in my body, sitting on my cushion. As soon as thought entered my mind, I was snapped back into my normal state of consciousness, and lost was my oneness with all creation.

When I came out of meditation, I felt energized and restored. Every cell in my body felt as though it had been washed clean. The knowledge was now with me that I was well, that the cancer no longer held residence within me. I knew in an instant and beyond all doubt that it would never return. That was over twenty years ago, and I am blessed to say it has never come knocking since.

Once you have become transformed through Divine Realization, the "old" you is left behind and illness falls away. The new you is exactly that. The disease that once held residence in the old you no longer has a home, as through the grace of evolution, we have left behind our wounded selves.

In the new, improved version of oneself, there is no longer anger, regret, depression, fear, or perhaps self-loathing. With the release of those negative emotions, our bodies are washed with Divine Realization, and the negative, disease-ridden consciousness no longer resides within us. When those negative charges are released, we become whole and health is restored.

But where did I go so deeply in my meditation? It was beyond any experience I'd ever felt before. It felt as if I'd traveled to another realm, another plane of existence beyond our everyday lives. There was no Earth, no sky, and no people, yet I was not alone. There was simply an incredible state of being, one and the same with vibrating, pulsating life energy. I was completely relaxed, without care or worries. It was as though I was being carried along in one vast ocean of consciousness.

Dr. Bryan L. Weiss, a renowned psychiatrist and author of *Many Lives, Many Masters,* relates a session he had with one of his clients. Under hypnosis, Dr. Weiss's patient could go to what he termed the "in between." She described herself as "floating" when she was in that consciousness. Dr. Weiss wrote, "Once we had stumbled into this new realm, her improvement was dramatically rapid, without any medicine. There is some powerful curative force in this realm, a force apparently more effective than conventional therapy or modern medicines." *Was her state of consciousness the same one I had experienced? Had we gone to the same "place" to receive our healing experience? Was her experience she described as "floating" the same as my experience of moving forward in the waterless river?* I was left wondering.

July was upon me, and the end of my healing summer was fast approaching. I was now well, and although it was difficult to imagine going back out into the noisy world on a daily basis, it began to dawn on me that I needed to get back to work to bring in some income.

As luck would have it, it was also one of the hottest summers on record. Temperatures were consistently over 110 degrees for several days in a row. Funny enough, as soon as I started thinking about my dwindling money, a negative thought, there was a negative result: My air conditioner broke. I realize now that my trust had faltered. I had remained worry-free all summer, and everything had gone smoothly, but as soon as I allowed concern to enter my world, cause for concern manifested.

I called a repairman and described the symptoms, and he was ready with an answer. He quoted a fee, based on what he thought the problem was, and said he could come first thing the next morning. Though his quote for repair was level with my bank balance, I hesitated but invited him anyway.

All day long I vacillated back and forth between worry and trust. More times than I like to admit, I had the urge to pick up the phone and tell the repairman not to come. The cost to fix the air conditioner would virtually wipe out my liquid funds, and I wrestled with that fact all day long. That evening, I knew a decision had to be made, as the repair service was about to close, and they'd be at my doorstep in the morning, before I could call to cancel the next day. I got into the shower at four forty-five, knowing the business closed at five. I struggled—back and forth, back and forth, back and forth. *What should I do?* I finally exhausted my mind enough that I was able to weigh the incredible gifts I'd been given during my weeks of seclusion. *Has God failed me once? Have I learned nothing? Has He not been trustworthy above all expectations? Have I not seen how He has taken care of all my needs?*

As I wrestled with all this, I sank to my knees in surrender and muttered, "Trust and believe," out loud. This is no exaggeration: As I released my worry to God with that utterance, the phone immediately rang. In fact, the last word, "believe," had barely cleared my lips when the ring of the phone shot through me. Dripping wet, I picked up the phone to hear the familiar voice of my soon-to-be ex-husband on the other end.

He had been traveling with his latest movie assignment, and he'd returned briefly to our area. I had not spoken to him in four months, so it was strange that he called to check in with me—not to check *up* on me, but to check *in* on me. Anyone who knew the depth of dispute between us would have realized how uncharacteristic and abnormal that was. I can only tell you it was entirely unexpected.

We talked amicably for a few minutes, and he turned the topic to the unseasonably oppressive heat spell we were experiencing. He told me it was slated to hit 112 degrees the next day. I told him I was aware of that, and I mentioned that my air conditioner had just gone out. Knowing I hadn't worked in a while and that I'd been ill, he immediately asked if I had called a repairman and if I had gotten an estimate of the repair cost. When I told him, I was amazed at the level of concern he expressed. In the past he hadn't seemed that concerned about me even in the best of our times together. He told me he wanted to come over that evening to give me a check to cover the cost though the thought had never even entered my mind to ask him for money. Needless to say, I hung up the phone in a daze.

When the doorbell rang, I opened the door to find him standing there extending a check out to me, written in the exact amount of the blind quote I'd received from the repairman. He assured me that I didn't need to repay the money and, then he left, just like that. I had no choice but to believe it must have been God Himself who had handed me that check through that man with whom I'd shared such a damaging relationship.

Bright and early the next morning, the repairman came. When the bill was presented, I needed only $1.08 of my own money beyond that check from a seemingly most unlikely source, my estranged husband.

It was either the man I had thought my ex-husband to be when we first married, before his problems became evident, or it was a divine force working through his physical body. Famous evangelist Billy Graham spoke about how God sometimes uses ordinary people to do His good works. I couldn't help but wonder, *Was that really my ex-husband or an angel in disguise who rang my doorbell and handed me that check?* Whatever the answer, I sent out my gratitude to both.

> *"Healing is not forcing the sun to shine but letting go of that which blocks the light."*
> **Stephen Levine**

# CHAPTER 5

## The Soul's Prescription

**FLASHBACK**

It was in the middle of the night, and my ex-husband and I had had an argument that turned ugly. For the first time, I'd driven myself to the emergency room at a nearby hospital. Due to the late hour, I had to speak to someone at an outside window, like a drive-thru window at McDonald's. When asked why I was there, I made some feeble excuse about why I thought I needed to see a doctor. The woman behind the glass studied me closely for a few seconds, then picked up the phone and dialed. While the phone was still ringing, she extended the phone to my car window without saying a word. When the ringing stopped and the voice on the other end of the phone answered, I realized she had put me through to an abused women's shelter, where she hoped I would seek help. I didn't say a word when they answered the phone. I simply handed it back to her and drove away in a more dazed state than when I had arrived. At the time, I didn't mention the incident to anyone.

I also never mentioned to anyone that when we stayed at the Savoy Hotel in Italy, during an argument, he grabbed my hair from behind, wrapped it around his fist, and forced me to bend forward at the waist with my face toward the floor. I was still on my feet as we stumbled forward in that painful, precarious position into the bathroom. I had filled a deep European tub to the top with hot water in anticipation of a long, up-to-my-chin soak, but I now innately sensed that I might be drowned as a result of his drunken craze as he pushed me toward the filled bathtub and held my head low. I screamed for all I was worth, summoning the blessed knock that came on our suite door a few minutes later. Needless to say, I returned from Europe to Texas alone.

I'd also not shared the story about the time when, after three margaritas, he sped away after literally kicking me out of our moving vehicle on the highway, leaving me alone in the middle of the west Texas desert. At least he'd had the courtesy to slow down first, allowing me to avert more serious injury. I didn't mention my shame and embarrassment when the car in the distance behind us saw what had happened, nor did I tell anyone about my relief and gratitude when that young man stopped to render aid. I certainly didn't talk about the guilt I felt when my ex-husband, who had evidently been watching his rearview mirror, turned around, drove back to where I had been ejected, and threatened the man's life for daring to help me before he forced me back into the car. Luckily, it was only my naiveté that died in the desert that day; it very well could have been me. There were other incidents, but you get the picture.

I told no one of these experiences with my ex-husband. Even

my family didn't know all the details of our sad relationship at the time when all this was going on. Since few details were shared by me at that time, they knew my husband had become "abusive," but that was an umbrella word, and we lived 1,200 miles apart. For the most part, until I opened up to my sister, those incidents from my previous marriage remained private. I was subsequently lucky enough to marry someone who was very happy just to pick our lives up from the moment we met and move forward. There was not a lot of delving into the past by either of us. We just accepted what the other one wished to share, and we never looked back.

The only reason I'm sharing my experiences with you today is in the hopes that you'll seek outside help if you're being abused. If I didn't share these pieces with you, I couldn't give hope to those of you who may be experiencing physical violence. I can bear testimony to you that there is life beyond, perhaps even a beautiful life, waiting for you to seize it and make yourself available to it.

During that short marriage, my ex-husband often said he was sorry and made promises to get help, but those promises were quickly forgotten, and the violent scenario would repeat itself. The one or two times he did seek help, he checked himself out of rehab after only a few days. He denied using drugs and being an alcoholic, as most addicts do. If you are in this predicament, I ask you to seek outside help. Trust me when I say it is nearly impossible to turn things around yourself, even if you think you can. Men cannot hear the voice of reason from the women they are abusing. The way I turned things around in my personal life was by returning to my relationship with God, and that led me to safety and healing.

That short, tumultuous marriage was the learning curve of my life. I wondered, *How did I ever get myself into this life-threatening madness? What's more, what am I going to do about it?* I left him again for the very last time after I was diagnosed with cancer for the third time in ten years.

What did I learn from that abusive relationship? Not until we find the strength and courage to move *out* of our lives that which is not working will we be able to make room for and welcome that special something that *will* work in our lives. Until we reach deep down into that well of strength that we all house within and until we exert the necessary courage that is housed within each and every one of us, our spirits cannot rise up, nor can they soar, and we will remain stuck in our powerlessness.

If you're currently in an abusive situation, I urge you to check out in advance the shelters you can retreat to the next time these behaviors repeat themselves. I never did that, but I know if I had, I wouldn't have stayed in my short relationship even as long as I did. In order to eject ourselves from an abusive situation, we must learn to take control of our own minds by making deliberate decisions. Checking out a shelter or simply driving by one to imprint its location, just in case, is an excellent way to begin.

When we're trying to cope in those instances, our vision is unclear. Emotions can blind us. If you're going to run for assistance, don't just merely go to your family or to a friend's residence. Go someplace equipped to truly render assistance to you, or you'll get stuck in that cycle of leaving and returning.

God may only open the door of escape a crack, but it is our duty to run through that crack and burst the door wide open when the opportunity arises. Belief in oneself, one's destiny, and one's higher purpose is the only fuel that can ignite the engine of exit. Believe me when I say to you: If I managed to turn my life around, you can too. Believe, believe, believe! Trust and believe!

At the end of my summer of renewal, after spending time in seclusion, I knew the way to finalize my relationship with my ex-husband was to do just that: to finalize it! Without telling him why, I asked to meet him in person, without attorneys present. The first thing he wanted to know was what I wanted, and I told him the truth: I just wanted it to be over. That was all I wanted. I just wanted it to be finished, once and for all.

I walked out of that relationship with the car I had bought and paid for prior to our marriage, with my personal belongings, and nothing more, but I was happy! I was free and felt as though I had handled it well. I didn't fight for our home, and I took none of our assets because I had the greatest asset anyone could ever ask for: I had God on my side.

The first order of business was to gain employment, as I needed an income. I didn't want to go back into the same type of employment I'd had for so many years. I sought a lighter, less-encumbered lifestyle, a job that wouldn't require me to work excessive hours every week. My meditations became a question to the Great Provider: *What should I do next?* I would pose this question every day before sitting in quietude, waiting for the answer to come. Fortunately, I didn't have long to wait.

One of my friends worked in an advertising agency. I knew nothing about advertising, but I remember thinking it would be a fun change to work there. The employees were allowed to dress casually, and once when I had visited her in the office, there had been color, beautiful color, throughout the entire building. How refreshing it seemed for there had been no color in my previous workplace, just black and white. The law had been so drab.

Still, though I might have had an in had I contacted my friend for help, I was not quite ready to make contact with the outer world, so I decided not to call her. Instead, I decided I'd work with the Universe to manifest employment there. The agency's name had just been four initials, but I couldn't remember what those were. I tried to concentrate on the letters and magnetize myself so I could attract a job from the building interior. I thought the name started with a G, so I began there. I sat down on my cushion with intention. Before my meditation, I envisioned the office to which I had only gone once. I saw the colors on the walls and the casually dressed people as they bustled about with papers in their hands. I envisioned myself among them. I tried to see the letters with the name of the ad agency in front of the building, but the letters wouldn't come. In total exasperation one day, I looked up at the ceiling and exclaimed: "*You* know what I mean!" It was in that moment I knew beyond a shadow of a doubt the Universe could interpret our intentions.

After doing this practice for several days, I decided the time had come for me to get back in circulation. I began to have occasional lunches with friends, but it was hard for me to leave my cocoon. Just to do something different, I worked a temporary job. Although it was still in law, it was for an environmental firm, and I liked it. It wasn't long before my phone rang with an offer for fulltime, permanent employment with them. *How fortuitous!* I had just barely left my house, and after a summer of fasting, the Universe was filling my plate with opportunity.

The employment wasn't in advertising as I'd envisioned, but it was an improvement, a position with a prestigious law firm that specialized in environmental law rather than the heart-wrenching child custody suits I'd worked on in my previous job. Thankfully, I would no longer need to keep a box of Kleenex in my desk.

I interviewed for the position, and when I did, I felt as though the room was full of unseen supporters. I noticed that my countenance was completely different than it had been in the past as I had been shy, and my new sense of confidence surprised me.

After my secluded summer of meditation, my new sense of calm and purpose was so tangible that it permeated the very air we were breathing. I had never been so self-assured, and I noticed that my interviewer's hand trembled slightly as she handed documents and forms to me. My calmness had evidently begun to unnerve her, as she seemed to have gotten nervous since our interview began, but I knew I wasn't going to take the job unless it was what I wanted.

Each of the requirements I presented was amicably met. We quickly reached an agreement on salary, working hours, and benefits, and I was told I could start on a permanent basis right away.

The Universe had paved the way for me. The Most Benevolent had guarded and guided me like a shepherd cares for his sheep. The only problem I had was internal. It was a shocking adjustment to go from the schedule that was created for me in quietude to a full-time job, spending all day in a busy office with so many people and so much noise to invade my world.

Each day as I worked, my yearning desire to spend time with the Great Consoler was so strong it was almost painful. Then one day it hit me: By constantly wanting to be with Him, I *was* being with Him. It was not the intimate way as I was with Him when I sat on my cushion at home and had quiet and peace around me, but at the same time, I realized He was with me at all times, not just when I sat to meditate.

I then realized the necessity for balance between my spiritual life and the life I'd come into this world to live. I couldn't stay in my cave like the Yogis in the mountains of India. I had to step up to the challenge the Universe put before me. I needed to continue to *evolve*. Taking these words to heart, life began to improve for me, and it has only continued to get better.

*"When you follow your bliss—and by bliss I mean the deep sense of being in it and doing what the push is out of your own existence—you follow that, and doors will open where you would not have thought there were going to be doors and where there wouldn't be a door for anybody else, and there's something about the integrity of a life, and the world moves in and helps."*
*Joseph Campbell*

**ENTER MICHAEL**

Remember that friend I mentioned who worked at the advertising agency when I was trying to conjure up a job there? Michael worked at the same agency whose initials I couldn't remember in my meditation. I had not conjured up a job at all, but I did seem to have conjured up my soulmate!

When I'd fallen into my would-be tumultuous relationship with my ex-husband, I didn't consult the relationship road that always showed me the eventual outcome of my choices in previous relationships. When I looked ahead through the vapors of time, I always saw the road eventually disappearing, as if into a thick bank of fog. Although those relationships seemed to be working fine at the time, somehow I innately knew the partnerships were not meant to be forever. When I married my ex-husband, I didn't consult the road because I didn't want to. In that case, I only wanted what I wanted when I wanted it. Choices based solely on wants will always lead us down the wrong path. Had I consulted the Source that had always served me well, I would have seen that that particular pairing would not dissipate into the softness of the fog as the others had. I would have seen that that relationship was going to slam me up against a brick wall.

When I met Michael, in consulting my relationship road, what I saw was the reassurance I needed. It was as though I was viewing the road from a helicopter hovering above Earth, watching the road stretch out in beautiful curves. All the other roads had been flat and straight, as though I was standing on the centerline and looking straight ahead. Until I saw the road for him, I hadn't realized the previous pavements had always been a dull gray, and each road had fallen into disrepair along the sides as it stretched out before me.

Michael's road, from my first ever-elevated vantage point, was newly paved, nice and black, with freshly painted yellow stripes not only up the middle, but also along its perfectly manicured, wide shoulders.

It snaked along the most beautiful, winding coastline, where waves lapped upon the shore, much like the majestic California coast. It wound through the mountains and came into the desert in bloom before climbing back into the mountains again. As the helicopter of my mind continued to follow and reveal our future, the road continued on and on. I followed it for so long through the beautiful vistas, beside streams and forests that it eventually disappeared over the curvature of the Earth, much like the road does in the famous Bonneville Salt Flats of Utah. The area there is so flat for so many miles in the distance that you can actually see where the Earth begins to curve downward to form the round planet on which we live. Michael's road wasn't flat, and it didn't end; it simply wrapped around the Earth. I knew then that it was to be the relationship of my life.

When I met him, I wasn't ready to go into another serious relationship. Thank goodness he was patient with me, and so very persistent. Before we married, my parents were concerned. After my fiasco of a relationship with my ex-husband, they were understandably wary, especially since they lived so far away, and they couldn't verify my wisdom or lack of it. I distinctly remember having a conversation with my mother one day on the phone. She asked, "Are you sure, Ginny?" I told her that, because I was still holding trauma from my past relationship, my mind was telling me to run as far away as fast as I could, but my knowing was telling me that if I married Michael, I would be happy for the rest of my life. I had to honor that wisdom within me, the knowing that had nursed and directed me through my illness, had guided me to realizing the quickest way to end my previous marriage, had led me to stable employment, and a thousand other things for which I had not given credit where credit was due. I explained to my mother that in my previous marriage, I had acted on impulse and had pushed my knowing aside, but this time, I was acting on my knowing, pushing aside the impulse to run. It was a challenge for me to be led into a new relationship by the Powers-that-be, especially so soon after my previous relationship had ended so badly. I told my mother that the relationship with Michael came from my deepest knowing.

After that conversation, my parents were very supportive, and when they met Michael, they saw what I saw. We married within a year of meeting each other, and twenty-plus years later, I now know it was the wisest decision I've ever made.

When we began dating, we'd meet after work and walk the running trail that stretched in a ten-mile oval around our tree-lined, downtown lake. It allowed us the time we needed to decompress from the busy lives we lived while apart. Those walks were a welcome time to talk and reflect on our day, but since Michael is the quiet type, many times, we would just walk in silence, enjoying nature and each other.

One day, while walking on the trail, discussing our spiritual views, he made the oddest comment: "I'm not sure, but I think I might be an atheist." That got my attention, and I knew that comment would be filed in my mind in big bold letters: *ATHEIST?*

A few days later, we were walking and talking about our parents. His mother and stepfather had been killed in a head-on collision by a drunk driver on the way home from eating dinner in a nearby town, when their car had burst into flames. After the funeral, he had gone to his stepfather and mother's farm, with his brother and sister. Seeking solitude, he'd walked out the back door, to the frozen pond beyond. He said it was extremely cold that day, and as he traveled the path, a small sparrow huddled in the middle of the walkway. Sitting without flight, watching him as he approached, it allowed him to pick it up. Not knowing what to do with it, the three of them decided to put it in a shoebox and transport it from the farm to their mother's home in town, where they were expecting friends and family to gather after the funeral services. The intention after the gathering was to somehow nurse the small bird back to health or find someone who could.

At first, the bird seemed calm and traveled quietly in the box, but during the drive from the farm to their mother's home in town, they had to pass the same exact spot where the accident had happened only a few days before. As they approached the accident site, the bird became alarmed and started flapping and beating its wings against the box so violently that they feared it might injure itself. They slowed the car, opened the box and the window, and set it free. He then said when he had carried that bird in his hand from the pathway on his way from the pond he had felt that it was his mother's spirit, letting him know that she was still with him. Needless to say, I knew beyond a shadow of a doubt that the man who walked beside me on *that* pathway was no atheist.

Michael has been very successful in his career, well known and well respected, and he has always provided very well for me, thanks to his unending generosity. After we married, I continued to do my spiritual practices, and soon he was steeped in my spiritual journey. It was not long before he began to abandon the television downstairs; instead, we read books together in a large, sunlit room he had converted into a space specifically designated as my own so I could have quietude and peace for my meditations and studies.

During my summer of healing, before I went back to work and met Michael, I had made a pact with God. I proposed that if I didn't have to work anymore, I would dedicate the rest of my life to Him. I would spread the word, verifying His existence in my life and in the lives of others, letting them know that He, the most Benevolent One, is not some far-off and distant God somewhere as far away as Heaven, but He is right here with us in each and every moment, guiding us and watching over us.

I've tried to keep my end of the bargain, and I suppose that's how this book came about; this work that seems to be writing itself as my fingers press keys without knowing what the next words will be. This is evidently another of God's parts in that pact I made with Him all those years ago. He seems to be helping me to get the word out.

Even though our lives were full and happy, I couldn't shake the familiar nudge that was telling me that something might still be missing. I decided to go to that same familiar metaphysical bookstore in the hopes that if I just wandered up and down the aisles, something would jump out at me. I hoped maybe something would speak to me or guide me to my next step. Walking in the incense-rich rooms, I browsed and allowed the peaceful atmosphere to engulf me. While I roamed up and down the aisles, waiting for a sign, a short distance ahead of me, a book fell from the shelf for no apparent reason. I assumed someone had replaced it haphazardly on the shelf, and that it had succumbed to gravity. I walked ahead to replace it on the shelf, as no one else was nearby, and when I bent to pick it up, my eyes met the eyes of the woman on the cover. They were deep brown eyes that engulfed me and left me swimming. The cover was orange, as were her clothes. She had long, wavy, black hair and a face of unusually radiant and inviting countenance. When my eyes left her face and took in the title, I knew I'd found the next step in my spiritual quest.

The title was familiar, as it was the very book that had been first on my energy worker's list a few years earlier. It was the book I hadn't bought and read because it hadn't called to me then, though I had read the others on the list. Now, this book would give me new direction in my life. *Autobiography of a Yogi* answered my question about where I was to go next, and it turned out to be the book that bonded our marriage.

We began doing our spiritual practices together, as taught by this teacher. She was not really a *she* at all, but rather a *he*, with long, flowing black locks. He was also a fully self-realized guru from India, Paramahansa Yogananda. Our questions pertaining to life and the spiritual realm were answered in dazzling detail. It was also a deeply satisfying account of the self-realized soul's upbringing and unshakeable belief that God heard every word he uttered and responded in kind. As we pored over the words on those pages, I felt like I had come home.

Founded by Paramahansa Yogananda, Self-Realization Fellowship Headquarters is located in Los Angeles, California, and I wholeheartedly encourage anyone who visits that city to stop by The Lake Shrine gardens on Sunset Boulevard, near Santa Monica, just up the hill from the ocean. Not only is it beautiful, it offers a serene, deep peace right in the middle of the bustling city—a city you won't even see or hear amidst all the lushness that will surround you.

I personally know four who have experienced true transformation just by sitting in the lush greenery, among the thousands of flowers overlooking the private lake on the grounds. Many of those flowering shrubs and plants were planted by Yogananda, himself, after he had them shipped from all parts of the world to this beautiful retreat.

On the property is also a shrine that holds a portion of Mahatma Gandhi's ashes. It is thought that the rest of Gandhi's ashes were scattered at sea and in the waters of the Ganges and Humuna Rivers. The ashes portioned out for the retreat gardens in California were a great honor for Yogananda; it was befitting, too, as Gandhi took initiation into Kriya Yoga through this great teacher. You will find that Self-Realization Fellowship is not a religion, but a path that compliments all religions. It was that path that cleared our way.

Over the years since we read Yogananda's book, we've done much research together on various spiritual traditions. The book offered us our first teaching by a self-realized master. It gave us direction and the knowledge that we are not just randomly passing through this life; rather, we are guided and led, if we will but listen. The autobiography changed both Michael and me for the better, and as it's taught today in many universities in their theology classes, it's not only a great read, but also a great learning tool.

I now know the reason I didn't read the first book on the list my friend gave me during my healing summer: If I had read it at that time, when my soul was so burning for more knowledge and a deeper connection with the Divine, I would have run off to California in a minute to immerse myself in meditation and study that master's teachings. Had I run off to California to join this organization at that time, I would have missed the opportunity to meet my husband. *Autobiography of a Yogi* was meant for us to read together, so I had to wait. The Universe is so benevolent!

I appreciate Michael more than words on paper can express. He is kind, gentle, generous, intelligent, capable, and creative and has provided me with the most wonderful life I could ever have imagined. It was hard to trust again, but when I did, the world was laid at my feet.

Friends and acquaintances have always complimented us on our marriage. When I'm asked about the secrets of a good marital relationship, if time allows, I sometimes share the following tips, which seem to be working for us thus far.

Although we certainly have our ups and downs, respect is mostly always shown to each other. I believe mutual respect is the basis of any enduring marriage. We also try not to say things we don't mean. This keeps our communication clear and un-muddled and keeps our trust intact. We try to stay on topic, without bringing in past disagreements or hurtful circumstances that don't apply to our current discussion. And, most of all, we realize that when we do disagree, it's just a moment we're having. When we do have those moments, they never change what's real between us. We know those disputes aren't what define our relationship with one another. In six months, we probably won't even remember what we were arguing about or that we had argued at all. So, in the big picture of life, just how important is this moment we might be having with each other? This type of thinking helps us keep our perspective. One other tip you may want to think about is whether it is more important to be happy or right. Sometimes in arguments, that decision has to be made as circumstances may not allow us to be both at the same time. If it is going to be successful, fulfilling, and enjoyable for both parties, marriage, like any relationship, is a compromise.

You might be wondering how my two marriage relationships fit together. Simply put, I know in the core of my heart that I wouldn't have the deep appreciation for my current partner had I not experienced living with one who was not as kind. I make sure to notice and appreciate every simple, caring thing Michael does, whether I verbalize it or not. Without the trauma and experiences of my previous relationship, I might not be able to recognize the scale of appreciation and gratitude I owe to Michael for his caring acts. It is through the caring heart of my husband today and through the grace of The One Who Sees All Things that I am able to write these words about regaining trust.

Three years after marrying Michael, I received an unexpected phone call telling me that my ex-husband had committed suicide in a most awful way: He had tied a plastic bag over his head and suffocated himself. His new wife had asked a friend to notify anyone who might want to know. Although the news was sad and unexpected, it didn't surprise me that he could have done such a thing. Sometimes we have to search for blessings when such things occur. Though it was a sad phone call, the blessing I found in that dreadful news was in the fact that he had not chosen to take his own life when we were together.

*"When we...go back into the past and rake up all the troubles we've had, we end up reeling and staggering through life. Stability and peace of mind come from living in the moment."*
**Pam Vredevelt**

# CHAPTER 6

## The Mirror of Meditation

Those of you who practice meditation have probably already reaped your own rewards and would have plenty of stories you could share. As for those who don't practice some form of quietude for at least a few moments each day, I encourage you to begin for your own sake and, as grandiose as it may sound, for the sake of the world. I am specifically speaking of mindful meditation, how to use what is already within us to make our lives happier, healthier, and more enriched, and how to connect with the Divine in everyday life. Meditation is simply the practice of being in the present moment, not thinking about our worries.

When asked how to meditate, I often tell people, "There are as many ways to meditate as there are people in the world." That's quite true. Though there are certain techniques that will still the mind faster than just sitting and waiting for quietude to happen, each tradition has its own way. I can give tips, but I encourage you to discover, through investigation, the precise method that works best for you, for there are many variables to consider. There are closed- and open-eye meditations, hands loosely clasped around the navel, open palms turned upward or downward on the thighs, ones with thumb and forefinger touching, sitting cross-legged or in a straight-backed chair with feet flat on the floor; and these are merely a few of the various postures from several traditions, and any might work for you.

You may want to enroll in a meditation class, as it's easier for some to learn in a group setting, led by an instructor, at a scheduled time and place. A class is often a win-win situation. Not only will you receive personal instruction in this endeavor, but you will also meet new people who are also engaged in and practicing it as well, a common interest you'll share. If you feel you can't devote your time to a class, you may wish to investigate on the Internet or buy a book on meditation to help you get started. In this age of fast-flowing information, we are, more and more, drawing the outside world into our own. As such, we're losing our ability to listen to the world within us, to learn important lessons from the vast amount of information in our own personal archives.

Today, Americans live fast-paced lives and are often preoccupied by the material. Many use meditation as a quick fix or a coping method to get themselves through their day. It's often used like a valve on a teakettle. When the stress gets to the point where the whistle is about to blow, some of us find that a quick meditation can bring the pressure down, if only for a short time.

Though this is certainly better than nothing, the true purpose of meditation is to form a direct relationship with the Divine. Gnosis refers to an experience of the Divine from within;

this is the true purpose of meditation. I refer to this union as the "faith relationship." If the faith relationship can become established, relaxation in our inner and outer worlds will follow.

Long-practiced in India and Southeast Asia, it has now been embraced by a large number of practitioners in our Western culture, and the growth continues. Masters from the East have awakened many of us in the United States to its benefits. Even The Beatles helped spread the popularity of meditation in the 1960s as awareness rose dramatically through a result of their meeting and following the great Master Maharishi Mahesh Yogi. Yoga centers are also commonplace today.

In words alone, one cannot articulate to another exactly what the city of Paris looks like. We can only give our own impression, our own description of what it looked like to us. Without seeing the city for ourselves, we can only surmise its beauty and uniqueness from what others tell us. So it is with our connection with our Creator. There is nothing more personal. Until we *know* for ourselves, until we experience our *own* gnosis, it's beyond description in mere words. When we sit in deep meditation, we realize the vastness of the soul; we become fully present and aware. There is neither past nor future. We will be wrapped in the reality of the unending now, and our minds will shift from turbulence to order.

Once you experience this, you'll never be the same. You'll never look at the world as you once did. The knowledge gained through this experience is too vast to be contained in any scope of thought or words. And what's more, although I described my own experience of gnosis during my healing summer, my experience will most likely prove to be entirely different from yours; each awakening is tailor-made for the individual. This is why I urge you to set foot upon the path of your *own* discovery. When we sit in meditation and make the connection with the Divine, The Great Mystery will eventually reach down through the mist and lift us up into the warmth of realization. We are not the body, the shell in which we live; rather, we are immortal souls, housed in the camouflage of mortal flesh.

Ralph Waldo Trine offers his description of this experience in the book, *Character-Building Thought Power*:

> The kingdom of Heaven is to be found only within, and this is done once and for all, and in a manner in which it cannot otherwise be done, when we come into the conscious, living realization of the fact that in our real selves, we are essentially one with the Divine life, and open ourselves continually so that this Divine life can speak to and manifest through us. In this way, we come into the condition where we are continually walking with God. In this way, the consciousness of God becomes a living realty in our lives; and in the degree in which it becomes a reality does it bring us into the realization of continually increasing wisdom, insight and power.

In *A New Earth*, Eckhart Tolle writes, "In a genuine relationship, there is an outward flow of open, alert attention toward the other person in which there is no wanting whatsoever. That alert attention is Presence. It is the prerequisite for any authentic relationship." In this Presence, Tolle also describes the perfect state for meditation and communion. We need to practice being fully present in each moment in order to have an authentic relationship not only with others, but also with the Great Unknown.

Leaving the ego behind clears the mind and promotes the stillness that brings renewal as we are drawn ever closer to our Creator. The ego keeps the mind engaged. This, in turn, keeps us separated from God. Mental conversations, or mind chatter, are thoughts, and as long as there are thoughts, the ego thrives. However, once we pass from thought to the Great Silence, the ego falls into a state of quiet, and we are finally able to find peace.

Perhaps you have doubts. Perhaps you say, "Well I can't possibly withdraw from the world and do that. I have to work and live and take care of my family." I understand this completely, but have faith that by carving out this time to reunite with your Beloved, your life will be more manageable, will flow more freely, and peace will begin to rule your days. Easier said than done? It may seem so, but again, by carving out this time to be with the Source that sustains you, time will avail itself where there was no time before, expanding to accommodate your needs, like a giant rubber band. Don't become caught in the web of fear and self-talk that keeps you from taking the time to create a better life. As Maya Angelou said in one of her presentations when I was privileged to see her speak: "Sometimes we need to take the time to withdraw from the thoughts that won't withdraw from us."

My challenge to you is that you will not become paralyzed by all the things you need to do in the world. Create a safe, quiet space for yourself, even if you have to get up in the middle of the night to do it. One of my beloved teachers had a large family and a very small house in India, so he meditated in a closet in the middle of the night. If the desire is there, the time will avail itself, but we must do our part to create that space in our world for deep communion with our most loving Father.

Fill your hearts to overflowing with love and gratitude. Prior to meditating, make a gratitude list and review all you are grateful for so the feelings of appreciation and blessedness will be fresh. The list might include your children, your husband, your job, restored health, or whatever or whomever is written in the diary of your heart.

If you have a picture of a loved one, you may use that also. Sit in quietude, sending gratitude to God for bringing that special person into your life, sending that love forth from your heart, from your entire being to the Universe. Be *expectant,* not in a way that creates thoughts, but as you would be if you'd just glimpsed an old friend in a crowd and you are waiting to see if your friend will reappear.

For those in serious crisis, speak to the Father/Mother, sharing all your troubles, and then go into quietude and trust and believe that you have been heard. Send gratitude in advance of the answer, and the answer will come.

Know beyond a shadow of a doubt that He hears your intention. His greatest desire is to share Himself with you. Invite Him with the same politeness you would extend to a much-wanted guest.

And lastly, you must be *patient*. Many do not keep at meditation long enough to receive any benefit. If S/He is silent, don't take it as rejection, in meditation or in life. When we don't get what we want, it's often because God has something better in store. Building your meditation routine takes persistence, time, and a lot of patience. Stay with it, for those ingredients are the very foundation of what is to come.

You need to see what works for you and what doesn't, until you can sit quietly for a period of time, even if only for a few minutes. Remember, I started with only five minutes at a time, but I did that often throughout the day, until I settled comfortably into a longer routine. I also began with an eyes-open meditation, with my hands cupped in a circle around my navel. As time passed, I fell into a more natural posture for me, and somewhere along the line, I realized I had begun meditating with my eyes closed.

Perhaps the most important thing I can say about posture is to keep your back straight as you sit in quietude. It takes but a short while to build your back muscles so this will be comfortable for you. If it helps, you may choose to sit in a straight-backed chair, keeping your feet flat on the floor and your hands lying in a natural position, palms upward, relaxed on your thighs. This is the Western meditation posture, and it may work well for you.

Meditation is something like playing the piano, in that it requires dedication and practice. Most of us could not play a successful piano concerto from the first time our fingers danced on the keys. Likewise, it truly does take time to sit purposefully. Whatever you do, be kind to yourself as you begin this adventure. From my own experience, I've learned there is no greater perfume to draw the Divine near than gratitude and deep yearning for communion. When we sit in meditation, we should open the door of our hearts to invite God to come in to be with us.

In the Sufi tradition, it is all about living with an open heart, turning your heart back to God. Like sunlight, the radiance of an open heart nourishes us and shines outward, touching others.

Often in life, we are emotionally wounded. We may be deeply disappointed in another's actions and feel wronged, rejected, or worse. Our hearts can literally turn away from God, hardening behind protective armor that has built up during life's many bumps in the road. Flowing love and gratitude from our hearts to the Divine or to the person who has wounded us breaks down the armor that we have protectively built around our hearts. These small acts alone free the heart, allowing a great expansion of love to fill the newly opened space left vacant by our retiring wounds. Not only are we able to give our love more freely, but we are also more able to receive it. Our hearts literally return from their turned positions, then open like flowers in spring.

If your heart has been wounded by a relationship that has come to an end, whether through discord or death, there is a simple way to cut the strings that might bind your heart to the heart of another. Often, we don't *want* to sever those strings that continue to entwine our heart with theirs, no matter how unsavory the relationship has become or how long we have been grieving. Some types of sadness can be emotionally addictive. Our brains may become hardwired with depression through unceasing visits to those sad memories. We may remain hopeful, until we find ourselves stuck when the other person has moved on without us. When the realization hits you that you are wishing for things to "be as they once were" between the two of you, it's probably time to use this practice. This is a signal that you are living in the past, and you can't create in the future if you hold onto the past. Remember, the only sure thing in life is change. Nothing stays the same forever. Relationships usually get better or deteriorate. If they continue without change, they stagnate. This can be true even in the case of a deceased loved one for whom we cannot stop yearning. Healing begins when we see a situation as it is, not the way we want it to be. When we see the realty of a painful circumstance, we can then take the appropriate steps to allow ourselves to mend.

To begin this clearing process, get into your meditative posture and give yourself a few minutes to settle down. Close your eyes, and for a full five-minute session, repeat these words over and over: "I release (insert name) to (his/her) highest good." Then again, continue to repeat for the full five-minute session, "I release (insert name) to (his/her) highest good." Feel the emotion that wells up within you while continuing your repetitions.

You may wish to add a visualization to do simultaneously while repeating the above mantra. If you decide to use these two practices together, I suggest that you repeat the phrase for a minute or so before adding the visualization.

Visualize yourself seated across from the other person, as though your chairs are facing one another, so close that your knees are about to touch. Your arms are relaxed and by your sides. See two beautiful ribbons, in the colors of your choice, extending from your heart to theirs. The ribbons are not taut and straight but slightly relaxed. Admire the colors and textures you have chosen. Perhaps a light breeze allows the ribbons to ripple with the soft current. Concentrate a few seconds on that heart-to-heart connection that is streaming through the ribbons between your two hearts. Notice that as your arms are resting comfortably at your side, you are holding a pair of scissors. Lift your arm without moving the rest of your body. With the scissors, simultaneously cut both of the ribbons that bind you together. See the ribbons severed, falling back toward your body. Feel the disconnection created by severing the ribbons that bound you together, the expanse of empty air between you. Feel whatever emotion comes up in you and continue to do so as you repeat the above mantra over and over. You may wish to practice this particular visualization again and again in each of your quiet sessions. As you do, you will probably notice the initial reluctance to actually cut the tie between you subside; it will become easier over time the more it is practiced. When I initially came up with this visualization for myself, there was a ripple of resistance when I used the scissors, but I have employed these practices in the past, and I can attest to their power.

At first, this process may be difficult. Your heart may not feel ready to let go, but I urge you to continue this at the beginning of each of your meditation sessions. Feel it deeply within your heart and know that, by releasing your hold on the other person in the relationship and wishing only the best for them, you, yourself will gradually experience release and be able to move on. Forgiveness is the pole that allows us to vault over these problems in our lives and the best part of all is that you'll begin to slowly experience the joy of wishing them well by releasing them to travel their highest road in life. This, in turn, will allow you to travel your own better path. The good vibrations you'll send out will all be reflected back to you, and your healing process will be well on its way. Just stay with it and trust.

Sometimes when a relationship falters, we are left alone and consumed with vengeful thoughts of punishing the one who has wronged us. Please realize that holding negative emotions is not only a waste of time and energy, but it may also be a waste of our good health. It only serves to hold us back. When we can cut the ties, whether these are feelings of longing or revenge, we will be released, finally able to move forward to create a new and better life for ourselves. Paraphrasing Deepak Chopra, we should use memories, but we must not allow memories to use us.

In *Enter the Quiet Heart*, Sri Daya Mata explains:

> When I see people whose minds are troubled by so many problems—frustrations, unhappiness, disappointments,—my heart aches for them. Why are human beings plagued by such experiences? For one reason: forgetfulness of the Divine [from] whence they have come. If you once realize the lack in your life is one, God, then set about to remove that lack by striving to fill yourself with the consciousness of God in daily meditation, the time will come when you will be so complete, so utterly fulfilled, that nothing will be able to shake or disturb you.

Please read carefully the stories I have related in this book about experiences or answers I've received when praying deeply to God or as I sat in meditation. Remember the yearning factor, that deep, deep yearning for a connection with the Divine. Know that your yearning will pay off; it may not be today or tomorrow, but it *will* pay off.

In meditation, persistence is essential. Never, ever, ever give up. You will benefit on some level, even if you're not aware of it. Remember expectancy: Await the Divine with faith, knowing in your heart of hearts that S/He will come in one way or another. Know that your intention is heard. Remember with conviction that prayers are answered. As you sit, silently invoke Him with the purpose of connection, a prayer without words or thoughts. All these ingredients will work as a catalyst to expedite your connection. Remember, prayer is when you talk to God, while meditation is when you give God the chance to talk to you. If you choose to speak to God, open up your heart and let the words pour forth, but when you finish your heartfelt conversation or prayer, sit in meditation and yearn for the Divine to join you.

Feel worthy! No matter what you've done in your life, no matter what words have been said to you to make you feel "less than," know that you are worthy in God's eyes. We are created in God's perfect reflection. This doesn't mean in our physical appearance; it refers to who we really are. We are souls living in flesh, beings far beyond our beating pulse. Our souls are alive and well at all times, perfect in the reflection of our Father. He doesn't judge us, we judge ourselves and we judge each other. He has His hand extended to us at all times. Often, it is only our own feelings of unworthiness that keep us apart, and keep us from knowing we are loved.

If you've made mistakes in your life, just remember that you're not alone. God doesn't turn His back on us just because we aren't perfect. If we were perfect, we wouldn't need to be here, in this Earth school, learning how to evolve through the challenges that have been put before us or that we may feel we have created for ourselves. Overcoming judgment, whether of ourselves or someone else, is the key that will set us on the path to where we need to go.

Whatever you have experienced, whatever you have done, whatever you have been told in abusive situations, remember this: You are worthy in God's eyes! He created you, and you are loved!

*"God responds not necessarily according to our merit but according to the depth of our longing for Him."*
**Sri Daya Mata**

When we swim with the Divine through our deepest meditation in His great ocean of consciousness, we will be filled with Divine Light. We will feel inspired to shine that light outwardly, to carry it like a flashlight in the darkness to others. Drinking in the new light will revive us, for it is refreshment to the soul. This light is then carried out into the world like a blazing torch, shining its contagious illumination through the boundaries of hearts and minds, shining light upon light through places still held in shadow, washing the population like a great sea, illustrating yet another version of God's words, "Let there be light." Ultimately, it becomes like a great wave, cleansing the world and its population, changing us for the better. Through this process, God cleans our hearts. They become purified, open to pouring out new compassion, sympathy, and empathy.

Once we have begun to meditate and have found our home in the Great Quiet, things begin to go more smoothly in our lives. We begin to feel more joy. Our burdens become lighter, and life becomes friendlier, offering more opportunities where there were none before. Jobs may manifest, a relationship you have been hoping for may come to fruition, your health may improve, and overall, life will get better.

Always remember the ultimate goal of meditation is union with the Divine. The other benefits follow automatically. I've been married over twenty years now, and Michael and I have a practice from which we don't deviate, no matter what the world throws at us. We meditate thirty minutes every morning upon rising and thirty minutes every evening, right before bed, without exception. Even if Michael has an early flight and we must get up at four a.m., we set the alarm thirty minutes earlier to allow our day to start with our meditation practice. If we know we have a late night ahead of us, we sometimes meditate before we go out. Then, when we get home, we do a shorter ten- or fifteen-minute session before bed, to ease ourselves into that spiritual connection before sleep. There have been a few exceptions where life's circumstances have interfered, like forgetting to set an alarm in the morning, and having to run out the door without allowing for this practice, but when the unexpected happens and we miss our meditation, our days go awry and we may have accidents or we're too short-tempered. On those days, the things that can go wrong usually do. As a rule, this doesn't happen when we start from a place of centeredness in the mornings.

In meditation, don't try to control your thoughts. Human beings have an average 60,000 to 70,000 thoughts a day. If we tried to control them all, we would spend our time as thought herders, trying to corral each unruly interruption on the still pond of our minds. When thoughts come, simply accept the existence of whatever is there and go beyond it, not by exerting effort, but by simply letting it slip away without acknowledgment. The more one tries to stop the thoughts from coming, the more one struggles; the more one struggles, the more fruitless will be the period of quiet. Accept thoughts as they arise but don't dwell on them. Let them sail by without grabbing hold of them.

Meditation in numbers can have amazing results. In the book *Maharishi's Programs to Create Heaven on Earth,* we find a clear example. In 1978, Maharishi Mahesh Yogi demonstrated the positive effects that transcendental meditation (TM) could achieve. He demonstrated that "one percent of the population practicing TM in any city reduces the crime rate and sickness rate." During the 1978 test he called his "Global Ideal Society Campaign," the crime rate was reduced on a global scale in 108 countries. The positive results of large numbers of meditators were so astounding that it became known worldwide as the "Maharishi Effect."

Although Maharishi has now crossed over, his practice continues. According to Jenne Ball, who writes for the David Lynch Foundation, in an article posted November 25, 2010:

As the nation experiences fear and uncertainty about its economic future, a quiet, unexpected phenomenon is spreading across the country. According to FBI reports, violent crime has fallen for three straight years, with the murder rate now the lowest in four decades. These statistics defy predictions; police authorities had braced for a crime wave expected to be unleashed by the recession, rising home foreclosures and social despair.

But in Iowa, home of the Maharishi University, Jenne Ball continued:

Every morning and evening in Fairfield, Iowa, 7 days a week, 2,000 volunteers from 50 countries and all races and religions come together to practice group transcendental meditation. Their endeavor, called the Invincible America Assembly, is based on the ancient tradition of maintaining large group meditations to neutralize negative societal trends. In the vicinity of unified awareness, hostile tendencies disappear.

This is according to the Yoga Sutras, compiled some 2,000 years ago by the venerated sage, Pantanjali. Since the start of the Assembly, scientists have monitored crime rates and other social indicators, tracking possible correlations between the number of meditators and societal trends. Some see the rising positive trends, such as the inexplicable drop in violent crime, as evidence that the group meditations are working.

Taking time each week to seclude ourselves with our Maker quiets the mind, opens the heart, and inspires us to live more peaceful, balanced lives. We begin to get acquainted with whom we are actually sitting, and the more comfortable we become with that relationship, the more we want to continue. Eventually, we come to know that He is with us at all times, and the presence of Spirit continues to invite us closer.

To begin, you must first choose a comfortable sitting position in comfortable clothes so you won't be thinking about your body; wear nothing tight that will constrict the natural flow of blood or breath, nothing that may make you uncomfortable, even for a short period of time.

Choose a quiet place or one that is relatively so. If there are no quiet places at home, try to choose a quiet time, perhaps before everyone wakes up, after everyone has gone to bed, when everyone has gone off to work or school, or any time of day when you will most likely not be disturbed. It may even become necessary for you to go outside. Perhaps you could sit on the grass under a tree in your yard or on a balcony or bench at a nearby park. The quieter the location, the deeper you will be able to go, until you learn to block out distractions.

I create a space for myself when I begin my practice. If it's during daylight, I darken the room, light a candle, and burn a stick of incense. I put down my prayer shawl and face a picture of Yogananda, one of my great teachers. Ritual can lend a sacred element that subtly lets your senses prepare for the quiet that's to come. If you like, place a small table in this space to hold anything you consider sacred or pleasant. If you're a Christian, you may want to put a crucifix or a picture of Jesus or Mary next to your candle or incense, if you choose to use either. You might prefer a small vase of flowers or a beautiful crystal or all of these things together. If you're of another faith, you may follow this example, substituting your own favorite or symbolic items. All of these preparations—lighting the candle and incense, drawing the shades, putting down a prayer shawl to sit upon—take little time, but that short period of time will allow your body and mind to settle, to withdraw from the outside world in preparation for going inward.

After you're dressed in your comfortable clothes and seated in your personal space at or near your altar, close your eyes. Open-eye meditation is possible, but we tend to think about what we see, so even though I began with an open-eyed style where I practiced being at one with everything, as I stated earlier, I now do my meditations with my eyes closed. This might be an easier way for you to begin.

Allow gratitude and appreciation to fill your heart to overflowing: gratitude for life, gratitude for the streams of sunlight that touch your face, gratitude for God's love, gratitude for your children (if you have any), or for pets, nature, abundance, a relationship, or the breath you took before reading these words. Gratitude opens your heart. Sit and feel the gratitude streaming from your heart to the Divine. Thoughts aren't necessary for you to do this. Experience the warmth of gratitude in your heart. Feel your heart expand as you allow rays of gratitude to travel outward, into the world and beyond. To keep thoughts at bay, it's easier to simply feel the essence of gratitude, without getting caught up in the memories or circumstances that have actually created the feeling. Take a deep breath and hold it for a few seconds. Allow yourself to steep in this essence for a few minutes. You may want to say a short, heartfelt prayer before beginning. For the sake of example, one of the meditation prayers I have created for myself is: "Heavenly Father, open the archives of my memory so I may live in humble gratitude for all of Thy gifts."

You may be experiencing a trial in your life and need direction. Your prayer may be to ask for an answer to your dilemma or to see your situation changed for the better. You may wish to get closer to your Father, the One Who created you; ask for that experience or express love or heartfelt need. Direct your prayer in whatever way you feel drawn, then let it go. Don't continue to dwell on problems while you're trying to quiet your mind. Surrender and give them up, at least momentarily, to the Great Listener. It is S/He who is in control of the Universe, not us. We're merely human.

Make sure your jaw is relaxed. Relax the muscles of your stomach and allow it to be at rest, without tension. Sit in your chosen position, whether in a straight-backed chair with your feet flat on the floor or sit directly on the floor, sitting yogi-style on your bottom, with your legs crossed, folding your feet back toward the sides of your body, and keeping your eyes closed. You may want to use a pad or cushion if you choose to sit on the floor. Make yourself comfortable, settle, and begin.

One method I liked when I first began was to concentrate on my breathing. Breathing naturally, without changing the natural rhythm of the breath, I would simply pay attention to my ingoing and outgoing breaths. When thoughts arose, I would let them pass like clouds in the sky, never chastising myself or getting attached to them; I simply returned to the awareness of my breath going in and out.

This may all seem overwhelming, but don't let your fear of all the steps force you to procrastinate or to give up on your plan to learn meditation altogether. These are only suggestions. Don't let the suggestions above overwhelm you. Simplified, the basic premise of meditation is to:

- Sit in a comfortable position, in comfortable clothes, and in the quietest place you can find.
- Turn the mind inward, away from outer distractions.
- Keep your back as straight as possible.
- Don't try to be anyone other than the person you are. Be the "real" you and know that you are safe.
- Relax into the moment.
- Send your silent message from your heart to your Creator.
- Know that you are not alone.

Create a regular practice and commit to do it no matter how you feel. Set aside a specific amount of time each day that you commit to your practice and continue meditating during this block of time each day. You may find that you want to extend it. In the beginning, five minutes may be adequate. Time has a way of tricking you in meditation. When you first begin your practice, the seconds may tick by at an agonizing pace, and five minutes may seem like thirty, but once you've gone beneath thought to the Great Quiet, you'll be amazed when your thirty-minute or one-hour meditation is over. When thoughts cease (or at least greatly decrease), your awareness of time will begin to fade.

Your mind will make all sorts of excuses at first: *I'm too tired... I don't feel well...I don't have time today.* Most frequently, we tell ourselves, "I'll begin tomorrow." Sitting in quiet is not a taxing event. You must come to an agreement with yourself. Form a mental contract, if you will, that no matter what the outer or inner circumstances may be, you will persist on a regular, daily basis, even if from time to time you are unable to meditate for the full amount of time you had set aside for yourself in your regular practice. Remember, as Remez Sasson said, "There is meditation with thoughts, and there is meditation without thoughts."

It's certainly all right to occasionally sit in meditation for a shorter period of time if your time is limited. Some meditation is better than none, but you shouldn't make a habit of shortening your time. Commit to do a little longer meditation next time and then do it. Persistence is the ultimate key.

Meditation is something like exercise, in that if too much time passes between sessions, it may feel as if you are starting all over again. If we continue to exercise, our bodies remain fit, but when we discontinue, muscle and tone disappears, and we have to start from Point A. Think of meditation as exercise for the mind, but remember that it is, at the same time, a vacation from thoughts.

As you learn to go ever deeper in your meditations, you may choose to leave some steps behind, and you may choose to pick up new ones as you learn more about meditation. Whatever you end up with, stick with it. If you are constantly changing your routine, your mind will be thinking about changing your routine! Find a regular practice that works for you and, as quickly as possible, continue to dive deeper through the waters of thought.

Clearly, when we're out and about in the world, perhaps on a lunch hour, and we have the opportunity to find a few quiet moments to share with our Maker, we're not going to be able to put on comfortable clothes, draw the shades, and be in our own personal space with our altar. If we're being called to go within, which often happens after we have tasted the sweetness of connection, it doesn't matter if we're on a subway or sitting at our desk; we can still have a moment of inner quiet that serves as rejuvenation until we can sit in the sanctuary of our soul in our sacred space.

These are merely suggestions for those who are not at all familiar with this practice. We must only be quiet and comfortable, to be our authentic selves in order to refresh our soul in the vastness of space within. We must remember to be kind to ourselves. Even a jumble of thoughts in our five-minute respite is better than a jumble of thoughts as we rush through our lives. Our bodies are receptive to our intentions at all times. When we make rest and renewal our intention, we'll benefit from that short period, even if it's on a subconscious level.

Once we go within and discover our true nature, our authentic selves, we no longer feel the need to seek the outward approval of others. We become confident, grounded, and capable of creating the new and improved life we seek; this, in turn, compliments the new and improved version of ourselves that will emerge. It is there, just waiting for us, behind the façade of the ego disguises we once held up in front of ourselves. In this state of authenticity, the ego drops away, and our avenues of connection open with Source, as well as with the public.

Through feelings of inferiority and low self-esteem, we often feel we need to be *more* than we are, but nothing could be further from the truth! Our souls are divine and perfect just the way they were created. They can't be charred by the trials of fire we suffer on this Earth plane because they weren't created here. Our souls come from the vast beyond, in a realm far superior to the negative earthly vibrations we create that scar our minds. We are sparks from the Great Perfection. We need to make room in our day to begin thinking of ourselves as such and meditation can open this door. Quieting our minds is like training a beloved puppy. At first, that pet may run around wildly, but over time, he learns to sit. The more we persist, the quieter the dog becomes, until one day, as we hold the leash in front of it for its walk, it comes and willingly sits all by itself, in anticipation of what is to come. We can leash our minds in this same way. It just takes patience and practice. When we can leash our minds, we will know how to sit.

> *"The soul loves to meditate, for in contacts with the Spirit lies its greatest joy. If, then, you experience mental resistance during meditation, remember that reluctance to meditate comes from the ego; it doesn't belong to the soul."*
> *Paramahansa Yogananda*

# CHAPTER 7

## Transforming Beliefs into Wisdom

For over three years, I made the commute between my home in Texas and a California university, where I studied spiritual healing and Sufism. Sufism is the inner, mystical dimension of Islam. What I learned transformed my thinking. I found that Islam is full of beautiful teachings, at least the way it was interpreted by my teacher, who traveled between Jerusalem and California to teach it. Many of the world's religions have the same teachings and values at their core. It's a shame that a few extremists, through erroneous interpretations, give the impression that *their* version is true. I was surprised to learn that Jesus is honored in Islamic teachings, and he is also included in Islam's line of prophets. In fact, the Qur'an speaks at length about Jesus.

I made many American friends while we attended that school. Some converted to Islam, and others didn't. Many were studying for the same reason I was: to squelch the fear that was rising in our country and in our own hearts, through the power of education.

## IN THE CLASSROOM

In my Spiritual Ministries class one day, my professor asked us to do an exercise with a partner. After she provided us with instructions, my partner followed through and gave me one tap on the center of my chest, then repeated the words we had been instructed to say: "Be Mohammad."

Although my eyes were closed, I immediately envisioned a beautiful scene with a deer and small rabbits and a lamb nibbling the ultra-green grasses at the foot of a lovely green hill, where a tree was casting shade. Flowers of every color blanketed the landscape. The birds were plentiful, flitting about, singing in great chorus. It was one of the most peaceful scenes I have ever encountered. The colors were so enriched and vivid that I felt as though I was looking at a scene from a Walt Disney movie. All of the animals and woodland creatures depicted in the scene were gentle. There was not a predator among them.

Suddenly, I felt as though someone had a comfortable grip on the back of my collar, as if I was being pulled backward and upward at a forty-five-degree angle. The scene I had been enjoying began to shrink in the distance. Soon, I saw the surrounding countryside and, beyond that, the nearest small town. As I continued to be drawn backward and upward, I then saw larger cities beyond the small towns in the distance. The oceans came into view, and eventually I could see the round shape of the Earth. As my backward ascent continued at lightning speed, I could see the whole planet spinning in space, and I could see the oceans and the landmasses as well. Then I was among the stars, released from my backward ascent and I felt as though I had become the whole Universe, floating and timeless. Finding myself at one with all creation, I was in a state of indescribable freedom. Time didn't exist in the never-beginning, never-ending vastness.

I am not sure what my Muslim partner saw when the exercise was reversed, when I tapped him on the chest as he had done to me, but afterward, when the teacher asked us to relate our experiences, my partner literally stumbled out of his chair before anyone began. Visibly shaken, he left the room. Though we had become good friends in our studies, I could never bring myself to question him in the classes that remained, but it was evident that whatever happened to him during the exercise was powerful.

Soon after that experience occurred, I was sitting with another one of my spiritual teachers in my class on healing. As soon as class began, we were asked to go into a quiet state for a few minutes. We closed our eyes and began to settle from the outer activity and rush of the world. As I allowed my thoughts to dissipate, I began to see a blur of purple and yellow swirling together. In fascination, I continued to watch as the colors mixed and mingled in my mind until they gradually gained clarity. I felt as though a hand unseen had plucked the head of a flower and placed it deeply inside my chest, where the heart resides. As the colors continued to come together into focus, I saw the largest, most beautiful purple and yellow pansy I had ever seen, but just as it came into clear view, the teacher called us to open our eyes so we could resume class.

Although I was sitting several rows back and the heads of several classmates had been partially blocking my vision prior to our period of quiet, when I opened my eyes again, there was a perfectly clear pathway in front of me. My teacher's eyes were boring into mine. It gave me a jolt, and it seemed as though all distance between us had disappeared. As I was held in his riveting gaze, I perceived a smile playing at the corners of his mouth, and his head began to nod almost imperceptibly, as if he approved.

I was confused and hadn't a clue what had just happened as the room returned to normal. *What did that flower mean? How did our eyes meet, as though everyone in the crowded room but us had disappeared? What did he find so amusing that he would smile at me slightly and nod his head, as though transmitting a sign of approval? Did everyone have this experience at the same time, or was it only me?* I never knew the answer to that last question, but I did find the answer to others.

The next day, on my flight home, I began to read from Music of the Soul, a class textbook that was written by Shaykh Muhammad Sa'id al Jamal, head of the Higher Sufi Council in Jerusalem and the Holy Land. The first words my eyes fell upon were: "Show the *flower* inside your heart so that anyone can take what they need, because everyone needs this fragrance. This fragrance is different from any other because it is *your* fragrance." You may say it was sheer coincidence that I was reading an explanation about a flower when I'd just had an unexplained vision of a pansy in my heart the day before, but to me, it was a demonstration of the great teacher's omnipresent ability.

In class one day, my fellow students and I were asked to go into silence with our eyes closed to end our spiritual healing class on a quiet note. Nothing pertaining to any Christian teachings had been mentioned all day. With my eyes closed, I was sitting in quiet reflection, and I had the distinct impression that Jesus was standing before me. It was so real that I felt I would be able to reach out and touch Him if I dared to open my eyes. Keeping my eyes closed, I sensed that He reached out and put the palm of His hand over the crown of my head. Even though I felt no pressure whatsoever on the top of my head, I was sure His hand was there. We were then told to open our eyes, and my teacher exclaimed before we adjourned, "We were very privileged in class today, for Jesus just walked among us."

## THE SPIRITUALITY OF PLANTS

Who among us can argue that the beauty of flowers adds an enchanting dimension to our world? And who can disagree that of the billions of tons of food we consume each year, the bulk of it is derived from the plant kingdom? According to England's pioneer ecologist, William Cobbett, as mentioned in *Secret Life of Plants*, by Tompkins and Bird, evidence now supports "that plants are living, breathing, communicating creatures, endowed with personality and the attributes of soul?" According to this book, science has confirmed that just as the Universe can read our intentions, plants can too!

In an actual scientific experiment, a plant was hooked up to a galvanometer. The researcher's (Cleve Backster's) intention was to burn a leaf of the plant to see if any noticeable reaction could be measured within the plant when it became threatened. What he discovered was profound:

> The instant he got the picture of flame in his mind, and before he could even move for a match, there was a dramatic change in the tracing pattern on the graph in the form of a prolonged upward sweep on the recording pen. He had not moved, either toward the plant or toward the recording machine.

He asked himself, "Could this plant have been reading my mind?" To further test the results of this occurrence, he got a box of matches and was determined to carry out the experiment. Again, coinciding with *only* the intent to harm the plant, there was another sudden surge on the chart. In a later test, going through the exercise of *pretending* he was going to burn the plant instead of *intending* to burn the plant, "there was no reaction whatsoever. The plant appeared to be able to differentiate between real and pretended intent." Other tests concluded in the same findings.

Of course, I knew nothing about the scientific experiments on plants until years after my own personal experiences with their incredible powers of communication. The following are some of my own experiences with plants and their mysterious possibilities.

Does it sound crazy to say that, for several years, I shared a special relationship with a hibiscus plant? The plant was only a youngster, living in a six-inch pot when I bought it, but it flourished. I didn't have a green thumb at that time, so each plant I owned had to be a survivor, and boy, was it! I have already shared my deep soul connection with the animal kingdom, but I mention the following experiences to demonstrate the extraordinary resiliency, intelligence, and spirituality that plants possess.

Years before I married Michael, I found myself without any animals for the first time in years. I'd recently lost my beloved German shepherd, and I'd been traveling extensively since then. I was planning another extended trip to the East Coast, so I placed several of my plants with a friend and her husband. My favorite hibiscus plant were among the fostered plant life.

Months later, I returned and went to visit my friend and her husband. To my surprise, the house was vacant and carried a vibration of discord. I later found out their troubled marriage had come to an end. As I turned to leave, I glanced at a long-forgotten plant that had been left on the front porch, nothing but a brown stick. My gaze then went to the pot, and I recognized it as mine.

That feeble stick of brown was the flowering hibiscus I had placed in someone else's care.

For the first time in years, I was living without pets, and the poor condition of the plant reminded me that we were both lonely. I scooped it up and took it home and showered it with the love I would have shared with my animals, had I had any pet friends at the time.

The plant became my focus for weeks afterward. I watered it, greeted it when I entered the room, and reassured it when I left. I stroked the stalk and encouraged it to regain its health, which it did. Oddly enough, sometimes when I entered the room, I got the distinct impression that if it had had one, its tail would have been wagging wildly. That hibiscus and I had definitely formed a special bond, a communion.

Still single, my life had gotten busy again, as most lives do. I placed the hibiscus pot outside on my sunlit patio and went back to business as usual. Hibiscus plants require a lot of sun and water, and I was pretty good at providing both.

During one particularly hot summer, I was in the kitchen making a special dish, and I was intent on making it right. Glass patio doors were across the living room, and I could see my plant sitting on the patio beyond. My concentration on cooking was suddenly interrupted by a voice inside my head, two simple, commanding words in a deep, manly voice. I looked out at my plant through the glass doors. Like a magnet, it drew me out of the kitchen and through the room, until I stepped through the glass doors. In the direct sunlight, I felt its soil and found it to be bone dry. In my amazement, I realized that those words could have come from none other than the plant itself, as I was totally alone. "Water me" was its simple, magnetic request.

From the *Secret Life of Plants* cover endorsement by Richard M. Klein, Professor of Botany University of Vermont (in the Smithsonian):

> If I can't 'get inside a plant' or 'feel emanations' from a plant and don't know anyone else who can, that doesn't detract one whit from the possibility that some people can and do...According to the *Secret Life of Plants*, plants and men do interrelate, with plants exhibiting empathic and spiritual relationships and showing reactions interpreted as demonstrating physical-force connections with men...

Research also supports the theory that plants communicate with *each other*. Cornstalks, for example, have been found to emit a series of clicking sounds at frequencies the human ear cannot hear. When tested, the corn roots in laboratory cornstalks were found to grow toward the series of clicks. When other plants were tested, they also seemed to communicate by sending and receiving information from their neighbors through clicking sounds.

*The Daily Mail* (UK) made the following observation of this same research: "While this study doesn't prove that plants are conscious, it opens up a new debate on the perception and action of people toward plants." Monica Gagliana, who oversaw this laboratory test, is convinced that "plants are not insensitive objects and should be treated as living beings in their own right."

My husband can attest to what happened a few years after we married. I'd had that same hibiscus plant for several years, and the two of us had formed a strong bond. We'd been away for three months, and my green friend had not received the care it deserved in my absence. Where that plant had grown strong and recovered to a height of eight feet, a mere brown stick remained once again when we returned.

Michael was about to discard the pot with the bare, brown stick in it, but I stopped him. Without any forethought, I told him the plant was still alive. He scoffed and told me, "You're going to have to prove it, or it's out of here." The plant evidently received his intention, for when I watered it well, spoke to it gently, and trusted that it could sense enough of the situation to handle the challenge, it came through.

A few hours later, while we were upstairs in our reading room, we both looked up simultaneously. We felt strangely drawn to go down and check on the plant, and what we saw stopped us in our tracks. There, near the base of the stalk, were two small perfectly formed, green leaves; they had sprouted in less than four hours' time.

To again quote the *Secret Life of Plants*, one of the scientists (Vogel) concluded that after conducting test after various test:

> A life force, or cosmic energy, surrounding all living things is sharable among plants, animals, and humans. Through such sharing, a person and a plant become one. This oneness is what makes possible a mutual sensitivity allowing plant and man, not only to intercommunicate, but to record these communications via the plant on a recording chart.

Earlier, I spoke about the merging I experience with animals when I feel their joy, their pain, or their hunger. Perhaps this theory would explain how that bonding process takes place, allowing communication with plants as well. To this day, I believe my heightened sensitivity is a gift carried with me from a prior existence in the ethers beyond, one I didn't lose at birth.

A few years later, I read about the famous and beloved botanist, Luther Burbank, who was able to coax the thorny cactus to eventually lose its thorns; he was thus credited with developing the spineless cactus. He reasoned that the cactus evolved with spines to protect itself. When he took away all threats and provided a loving, nurturing environment, over a period of time, the cactus no longer sensed the need for spines. Evidently, through his care and compassionate intent, Burbank convinced the cactus to give up its thorns.

We had a beautiful back yard with a small stone wall that divided the upper yard from the lower. To stage the beautiful blossoms, we intermittently spaced pots with our beautiful hibiscus plants along the top of the low wall. Of course, my special, resilient hibiscus friend outshone them all with the beauty of its display and number of blossoms. The flowers were as large as Michael's hand, and the color was beyond brilliant in the summer sun; one could almost feel the vitality and happiness emanating from it when you stood nearby. As strange as it sounds, as we admired it and I spoke gratefully to it, I could almost feel it swell with pride.

Scientists are now studying the language that occurs between the nerve cells in our bodies and plant cells. Research indicates that some form of communication actually transpires between the two!

In Machelle Small Wright's *Behaving As If the God in All Life Matters,* she speaks about the energy in plants and their place in the spiritual realm. She also mentions the nature spirits who watch over these plants. The ancient Hindu texts also refer to devas or nature spirits as deities who act in angelic ways to guard people, animals and plants, and help them to grow and prosper.

In *The Findhorn Garden,* by The Findhorn Community, there are also many references to nature spirits and devas. By working "in a collaborative effort between man, woman, and plants, under the protection of nature spirits at the Findhorn Garden," it was not unusual to find forty-pound cabbages, and pictures verified these phenomenal claims!

Although we never saw any physical "proof" when we enjoyed our gardening endeavors, we both sensed a strong presence emanating from within our own little Garden of Eden. From time to time, we talked at length about this presence while working with our plants in the yard. After reading about the community at Findhorn Garden and their work with what they termed "nature spirits," we decided to do some investigation of our own.

That one particular hibiscus was so stunning that we decided to use it to conduct our own experiment. I asked the hibiscus for its permission to take a picture of the nature spirit that evidently watched over and worked with it, and Michael got the camera.

The picture, film and not digital, was soon forgotten, as we tossed the roll in the drawer when it ran out. When we later developed the film and saw the picture, we were astounded. It was especially captivating since we'd totally forgotten about the whole incident, until we saw it at that moment. The only way I can describe it is to call it a "swirl" of vaporous energy. It was the same hue as the flowers, as though twirling among all the leaves and extending approximately six inches from the side of the plant and above it. It was evidently an electromagnetic field of living, vibrating energy. Even though we then recalled asking the plant for permission to take a photograph of the nature spirit or deva that worked with it, it was amazing to us to find an

aura of energy around the plant, much like those that surround people. The ancient Talmud teaches: "Every blade of grass has its own angel that bends over it and whispers, 'Grow...grow.'"

## SHARING OUR GIFTS OF GUIDANCE

I learned a very valuable lesson early in my marriage with Michael. We'd only been married a very short time, and we were on vacation in the Rocky Mountains, outside of Vail, Colorado. For those of you who have been there, you know what an incredibly steep grade the Interstate has in that area through the passes.

As Michael drove, I was buckled in at the dining table in our motor home, doing some writing. I remember stopping several times in the middle of writing to feel the speed at which were traveling. It seemed much too fast for me, although I didn't lean over to look at the speedometer. I went back to my writing, only to stop again a few minutes later with the exact same thought: *We're going too fast!* It was all I could do to stop myself from urgently shouting to him to slow down.

Too nervous to write, I decided to join him in the front like a copilot, all the while saying nothing about my feelings. When I checked the speedometer and saw that he was actually traveling at a safe speed, I realized it was only my feelings that were urging me to tell him to slow down.

After checking the speedometer, I realized I was situated

haphazardly in my seat with my armrest up, sitting sideways and facing him more than facing forward. I had also not yet fastened my seatbelt.

Suddenly, that familiar male voice came into my head, distinct beyond doubt. It was as though a telepathic message had been sent, and deep within the right side of my brain, that message had been received loud and clear. It was a mental message, much more efficient than anything that could be spoken from mouth to ear.

The authority with which it spoke didn't allow for questions. The voice was deep and calm, but at the same time, it carried such authority and urgency that I immediately complied. The voice commanded: "HOLD ON!"

I looked over at my husband to see if he had also heard it, but he continued to drive, showing no reaction. I silently swung my legs around to the front of my seat, put down the armrest, and fastened my seatbelt. As I took hold of each armrest, I braced myself. Then I waited. A few seconds, later there was a loud, explosive *boom,* and our motor home jerked to one side. While we were traveling at freeway speed, one of our tires had blown into shreds; we could only thank God that neither of us were hurt.

Thinking about what could have happened to us, had the incident been any worse, a wave of guilt washed through me. The sequence of events that had followed my silent warning took Michael totally by surprise. I had been warned, and I had prepared for the unknown, for whatever was about to happen to us, yet I had withheld that information from the one I cared for most.

That day, I learned that it's important to share my experiences, my knowing, for that warning was given not only to save me, but so that I could also help Michael as well.

Bryan L. Weiss writes, in *Many Lives, Many Masters,* regarding people who hesitate to share their clairvoyant experiences:

> Many had never even told their spouses about these experiences. People were almost uniformly afraid that, by sharing their experiences with others, even their own families and therapists would consider them odd or strange.

**YVETTE**

A woman I had not seen before would be coming to me for spiritual counseling, and in preparation, I did some of the common spiritual practices I do each time; I know that it's important when I counsel someone that I shake away the material world and enter into a sublime state, tethered to my invisible Guides of Good. That way, I can be an open channel. My ego is put on hold during those sessions so that the words that come through me may be spoken in purity.

My visitor appeared to be in her late twenties. We had pleasant conversation before she began telling me of her painful relationship in the past that had resulted in a pregnancy. Soon after her boyfriend departed, she underwent an abortion. Although she felt it was the right decision for her under her circumstances, she was still wracked with guilt and sorrow, even though a few years had gone by.

As we peeled back her layers of pain, she shared something she had never told anyone before: She had already named the baby girl that she had carried within her for that short period of time. She spoke to the baby and confided all her deepest feelings, as though her soon-to-be-daughter would understand her words. Now, the baby girl was gone, by my visitor's choice, but she could not let go of the memory.

Very soon after her abortion, her brother's wife became pregnant. When her niece was born, she felt an instant love for the child. She explained that the bond between her and the child was incredible, that they were extraordinarily close. She spoke of her frequently and wondered if she was so attached to that little girl because she had terminated the growth of her own daughter.

When I asked what she had named her baby, she didn't answer right away and continued to play nervously with a thread on her sweater. When she finally did reply, it was a simple, soft, "Yvette." I then asked what name her brother and his wife had chosen for their daughter. She looked at me a long time and finally repeated, "Yvette." Remembering she had never told anyone before me that she had named her unborn daughter that very same name; I chose not to chalk it up to mere coincidence.

I offer this to those who have chosen to terminate a pregnancy. As our souls are eternal, it is my belief that before we enter this comparatively short life on the Earth plane, we have chosen our assignment to work with certain people for the advancement of our spiritual growth. This agreement is somewhat like a contract in Earth terms.

I also believe there are times when an incarnating entity may, for whatever reason, choose to terminate that contract. Perhaps they've found a better choice for the assignment they have taken on in this lifetime. At such point, the pregnancy is terminated by miscarriage, by an occurring accident or mishap, by choice of the parent(s), or for health reasons that may threaten the life of the mother carrying the child.

To reiterate: In some cases, I believe it's not exclusively the choice of the parent(s) to terminate the pregnancy. In some cases, I believe it is the intelligence in the soul of the unborn child that terminates its choice to come into this world through those particular parents, for whatever reason. Again, this may be in the form of miscarriage, an accident, or a pregnancy terminated for other causes. Many times, the guilt suffered by the mother or both parents is unfounded, because the decision may have been made previously by mutual agreement between all of these souls before incarnating, or it may have been made by the intelligence of the embryo or fetus alone. That agreement, however, is on the soul level, not on the level of physical form and understanding.

Our children are not "mine" or "yours" like possessions we may own. They are God's children, not ours. They are individuals in their own right, with their own intelligence before and after birth, into this earthly realm. I believe that even before they take their first breath, they have their own life plan, and the parents they choose are the parents most likely to help them complete this agenda. Having free will, as we adults and children do in this lifetime, the embryo/fetus may choose to change its agenda for reasons unknown to us, and this may manifest in one of the above resultant pregnancy terminations.

Please understand that I'm not condoning or decrying abortion. I am merely saying that it's my belief that on a soul level, there is so much more at play than there appears to be or that can be comprehended in our mortal state.

If these words above comfort your heart in any way, I am grateful. If these words anger you, I most sincerely apologize. God, in His benevolent wisdom, allows each of us to have our own personal beliefs, and even if yours differ from mine, I honor them as much as I do my own. If you have lost a child, born or unborn, please know that my heart is holding yours as you read this. Time and distance do not matter, for we are all One.

I had never questioned the knowledge that had been placed

deeply within me as a child, but I did wonder occasionally if there were others that believed as I did. The theory of reincarnation was not among the teachings I had heard in traditional Christian churches so I held these beliefs close to my heart in my attempt not to appear different. It was a relief when I began to find books that supported the premise that we are not given just one chance to make it to what is termed heaven.

According to the theory of reincarnation, we are here more than once to learn in the process of our evolution. We are given lessons to learn and challenges to overcome in each lifetime, and with the successful completion of one lifetime we move on to our next assignment in another incarnation. If we don't successfully complete the tests in one lifetime, we are afforded the opportunity to learn those lessons again in a subsequent incarnation. We reincarnate again and again until we heal every aspect of ourselves - and in our truest essence, we become whole.

In *The Seat of the Soul*, Gary Zukov states:

> The personality and its body are artificial aspects of the soul. When they have served their functions, at the end of the soul's incarnation, the soul releases them. They come to an end, but the soul does not. After an incarnation, the soul returns to its immortal and timeless state. It returns once again to its natural state of compassion, clarity and boundless love.

This is the context in which our evolution occurs: the continual incarnation and reincarnation of the energy of the soul into the physical arena, into our Earth school."

## MY CHURCH

As I mentioned earlier, from as early on as I can remember, I've had a deep connection with whatever you wish to call it in your own belief system: God, Buddha, Krishna, Universal Spirit, Higher Energy, Nature, etc. I don't believe we necessarily have to go to a church with four walls to find this connection. I'd like to think I carry my church around with me, in my heart; I call it living with God, and when we live with God, we come from a centered place. My church is living in every faith-filled moment, and I am keenly aware that even in the darkest situations, God has a blessing for me. Living in this way enables me to go into my inner sanctuary at any time of day or night, without finding the doors locked because it's after hours.

As a couple, my husband and I consider our selves students of religion. We enjoy studying and attending various churches and hearing the many similarities in their messages. Sadly, however, many modern churches seem to focus more on their differences, and we find this approach brings separation rather than unity to the various faiths. Our faith doesn't necessarily fit into any one box. Our faith is what we call universal, and it comes from a place of deep commitment.

In this world, where things are so scattered, our energy is constantly being pulled in one direction or another. In these preoccupied moments, when we're focused on what's *around* us, we lose our connection to the Knower and our ability to recognize the guidance that comes from within.

We spend so much time living in our heads instead of in our hearts! When we're in our heads, we're thinking about what we have to do next, what we should have done differently, or where we have to be at seven. That breaks our connection with the Great Indweller. Think of it like a giant receptor, a radio station. When we're in our heads, the station has static and doesn't come in clearly, but when we're in our hearts, we're at the right place on the dial.

I am in no way suggesting that you should not attend church. The beauty we find within the teachings given by our pastor, priest, minister, preacher, bishop, rabbi, imam, reverend, etc. can be hidden treasures, guideposts in our lives. The unification of family, through church activities, is immeasurable, and church offers a social outlet, a place where bonding and lifelong friendships can occur. In fact, finding a church to attend when moving to a new location can be one of the best ways there is to become part of a new community and to feed the soul at the same time.

We often go to a non-denominational church, although we also greatly enjoy going to various other houses of worship, especially on special occasions. At Christmas, we prefer to attend a midnight Mass at the Catholic church, and we especially enjoy

Easter services, regardless of the church we attend. We go to the home of dear friends to observe and participate in their observance of Shabot in the Jewish tradition, and we like going to the Buddhist temple to participate in their celebration of the Chinese New Year. We have also joined friends occasionally at the nearby Hindu temple and others for Baha'i teachings. We enjoy and learn from them all.

As statistics have shown, there is a mass exodus of people leaving houses of worship and their structured religions to find their own way, an alternative way, instead of being led by a church official.

One thing that disturbs me is the hell-and-damnation sermons that paint God as a punisher. The God I know is a loving One, walking beside me and holding my hand, guiding me and protecting me, sharing His greatest secrets with me when I am ready to learn. Each of us must simply do what we feel is right for our own path through life.

> *"It is only when we forget all our learning that we*
> *begin to know."*
> **Henry David Thoreau**

# CHAPTER 8

## Simple Acts

**SERVICE AND DIVERSITY**

As a society, we're becoming more and more isolated with our long work hours, family obligations, constant electronic communication, worries, and responsibilities. Service work allows us to reach out and meet new people and broaden our views. It also encourages us to count our own blessings by comparison and often, the gratitude we receive from helping others feeds our hearts and souls alike. Helping others allows us to put ourselves in "other people's shoes," so to speak, and thus connect on a deeper level with our own humanity.

Through service work we have developed many deep, lasting friendships with people of various faith traditions. It has enriched our lives tremendously, and we have learned through the diversity we are exposed to while in service. Sharing and respecting our similarities and differences allows us to see life as a fuller, richer experience. It has been a tremendously valuable education, and no longer do we let the news media tell us their version of a culture. We have firsthand, deeper knowledge, and we can make our own appraisals through the teachings, integrity, and living examples of those with whom we interact. Kofi Annan, Nobel Peace Prize winner in 2001, said,

> People of different religions and cultures live side by side in almost every part of the world...We can reach out and love what we are, without hating what we are not. We can thrive in our own tradition, even as we learn from others, and come to respect their teachings.

We consider ourselves to be students of all faiths, and we love to learn. We are spiritual partners in this quest, for it is only through education, travel, and by welcoming diversity into our lives that each one of us in the world is truly able to broaden our thinking and to learn to be more inclusive, more tolerant, and ultimately, more kind. Even while pulling weeds in that community garden your town or city may have created, you will come into contact with people of diverse faiths, cultures, and views. I always have to laugh when someone asks my husband what faith he follows. His standard answer, without pause, is, "I am a Christian-Muslim-Hindu-Jewish-Buddhist." May the world be blessed with open hearts!

*"We are from different religions, but we are all from one Source, and we are all going the same place."*
**Paramahansa Yogananda**

## HEALING AND LIFESTYLE IMPROVEMENT

Many of us are going through life half-asleep, moving through our days in a dull-eyed, trance-like state. We are prone to becoming lazy and slothful as routine lulls our minds to sleep. Our clarity may fade, and our ambition may subside, leaving us without the drive to pursue anything other than getting through whatever the next day brings. Like sleep, this slips over us gradually. We forget our dreams in life, lose our joy, and a dullness of mind slips over us, sometimes so gradually that we don't even recognize that our natural vitality has diminished. Captured, we no longer live up to our potential. In this fog-like state, we stop living vital lives and forget to notice the gifts that are laid out before us.

How often do we take that commute to work and realize later that we noticed nothing along the way, that we have no memories of anything from our departure to our arrival? We lack stimulation by these repetitive activities. Many have forgotten to see the world and appreciate it, or, worse yet, have *chosen* not to see it.

In order to give our life meaning, we must guard ourselves from becoming mere automatons and reawaken our mechanical selves to more mindful living. We'll never live this day again, so let's make the most of it!

Try new experiences. Go to new places and change your routines; observe the faces that surround us or the nature outside the window as we move along through life. We need to reawaken our awareness and revitalize ourselves! Unfortunately, even when we *do* decide to change our lives, we often stay frozen in time because the thought of becoming revitalized seems too overwhelming. However, there is hope. Taking small, incremental steps, even in the worst of conditions, can lead us metaphorically out of our fog, into the warmth and vitality that a clear day and head can provide.

A plane ride is the perfect metaphor. If you've ever taken off in a plane during a storm or when a storm is threatening, you've probably had this experience. As you sit in the plane, waiting for takeoff, you see the darkness outside your window, when storm clouds cloak the sunlight. As the plane leaves the ground, you travel through those cloud layers, observing the dim light outside your window. As the plane continues its ascent, the darkness becomes filtered light, working its way through the layers until it suddenly breaks through the clouds into a clear day of sunshine and blue sky, leaving the clouds and darkness far below. In life, it's as though a weight has been lifted from our shoulders when we transition from immobility in our dazed condition to action and awareness.

> *"How many people are trapped in their everyday habits: part numb, part frightened, part indifferent? To have a better life, we must keep choosing how we are living."*
> *Albert Einstein*

That is what these few small changes listed below are about. Change is not so hard if we just take one small step at a time. As you will see, all of these steps are incredibly easy, as long as you have the will and determination to begin. Once we renew our zest for life, our forward movement begins again, and we are then able to reawaken to the joys in life. Begin, begin, begin!

1. **NATURE:** Getting out into nature positively impacts our sense of wellbeing and has been found to lift our spirits. It's a great stress buster and anxiety reliever, and you don't even need a prescription to receive these benefits. Research has shown that the calming effect of being in nature can also lower blood pressure through stress reduction. The peace it can bring is immeasurable, and it can often help clear our confusion when we are in need of a new perspective on life.

As you take your nature break, allow the fresh air to fill your lungs, the sun to shine on your skin. Employ and engage your five senses as much as possible. Smell the musk in the verdant soil or the fragrance of the flowers; listen to the bees busy at work, keeping our planet thriving with life, or to the birds messaging each other as they go about their day; taste the fruit from a tree or chew on a blade of grass; touch the bark of a tree and give thanks for the shade; look around and actually take time to see God's perfect creations, no matter how small, then bow your head in deep gratitude.

For all of us who live in urban areas, where we are constantly surrounded by concrete, asphalt, and steel, there is still good news. Studies have found that just viewing pictures of nature can also reduce tension and promote our sense of wellbeing. If a screensaver on your computer or a picture of a natural landscape on your office wall is all you have available to you, take heart: Even small doses of nature, whether viewed or experienced, have been shown through research to have a positive impact on our health.

2. **GROUNDING:** Webster's dictionary defines *ground* as "a conductor that makes electrical connection to the Earth." Scientific studies reveal that the human body is a living matrix, with electrons at the base of each living cell. Information is passed throughout the body via electrical impulses. Doctors sometimes measure the electrical activity of our hearts or brains through the use of an EKG or EEG, verification that each one of us is a living, breathing electrical power plant. If you doubt this, just slide your feet along the carpet and touch a metal doorknob. The resultant shock is a buildup of static electricity within the body, and grounding prevents this buildup of static electricity.

When our bare skin touches the surface of the Earth, we draw the energy of the Earth into our bodies through the Earth's never-diminishing electron fuel station. Even concrete, a product from the Earth, especially when wet, is a good conductor for this refueling process. Science has proven that the Earth recharges our bodies and brings them into alignment with the Earth's energy, causing a stabilizing effect between body and Earth. But what is the significance of this data? It's actually quite simple: The Earth carries a negative charge, and that's not a bad thing!

Damaging free radicals play a lead role in developing inflammation in the body. As studies are beginning to show, inflammation is now thought to be the very basis for all disease. Breakthrough studies indicate that chronic inflammation is the root cause of everything from heart disease, initially caused by inflamed arteries, to diabetes; from Alzheimer's disease to cancer; from arthritis to multiple sclerosis and chronic pain, to name only a few.

Damaging free radicals that might be ravaging our health by destroying and crippling healthy cells and causing inflammation to develop carry a positive charge. The Earth's healing electrons carry a negative charge. As human conductors, grounded by touching the surface of the Earth with our bare skin, the Earth's massive storehouse of negatively charged electrons pours into our bodies, ready to wage war. Negatively charged electrons then outnumber and overpower the lesser-numbered enemy troops of positively charged free radical electrons within our bodies, thereby reducing the root cause of inflammation. It becomes a matter of which electrons, positive or negative, have the most troops, the size of the human body or the size of our powerful Earth. Since science proves that electrons will always flow from a space where they are more abundant to a place where they are fewer in number, it appears that in every case, when we are grounded, the healing power of our behemoth Earth will always win this contest, reducing inflammation and decreasing resultant pain in the body.

As an example, try the following the next time you have a headache. To become grounded, remove your shoes, as they serve as an insulation barrier between your body and the healing energy of our planet. Stand barefooted, with your feet planted squarely on the grass or dirt for fifteen to thirty minutes, or if you have support problems, sit in a chair with your bare feet firmly planted on the ground. This will ground and center you even when your life is flying around you like a smarm of bees. If there is no grass, swim in the ocean or walk barefoot in the sand or on a beach or on the dirt of the Earth. If you live in an urban area without ready access to these, as I previously stated, even concrete, especially when wet, is a good conductor, provided you have bare feet.

As the soles of the feet have more nerve endings than any other location in our bodies, we receive a double-whammy when we connect with our world in this way. Though our feet form the best connection, we can actually receive the healing energy from the Earth when any portion of our skin comes into direct contact with the Earth's surface. Even if we live in an urban area or work or live in high-rise buildings, there is a solution, as grounding products can achieve the same result. The beauty of these products is that they allow us to become grounded while we sleep or sit at our computers or drive our car. It's that easy.

If you would like to understand this phenomenon better, I highly recommend the book *Earthing: The Most Important Health Discovery Ever?* by Clinton Ober, Stephen, Sinatra and Martin Zucker. They discuss the available products at length.

3. **SUNLIGHT:** As a population in general, few of us get enough sunlight. Many work or study inside all day, restricted by ceilings and walls. Even when relaxing, a growing number of us stay inside with our computers, televisions, and various electronic distractions. More and more often, we choose to sit in the comfort of our air-conditioned or heated homes, and the outdoors has lost its allure. As a result of this our health is suffering from these choices. Even hospitals have taken into account the value of sunlight. According to Matt DeBow in *Light,* "There is evidence that patients in well-sunlit wards recover faster than their counterparts in rooms with little or no natural light." Though there are many, the following is just one example of the benefits our bodies receive from sunlight versus one of the detriments of deprivation: Mr. DeBow continues, "The National Institute of Health discovered that limiting exposure to natural sunlight leads to a loss of muscle tone and strength." Whereas, "researchers have found [that] exposure to sunlight is similar to exercise in its effect on the body, improving blood pressure and increasing oxygen in our cells."

The sun is one of our most valuable natural sources of Vitamin D, a nutrient activated by the ultraviolet radiation in the sun's light. According to the *American Journal of Clinical Nutrition,* our nation is experiencing a pandemic of Vitamin D deficiency. "Studies have shown that 50 to over 70 percent of our population is deficient in this critical vitamin, and the cause for this Vitamin D deficiency is a lack of exposure to the sun." Who can argue, then, that sunlight is a crucial ingredient for healthy nutrition? It literally recharges our energy batteries! This is true especially in winter, when the days are shorter and work hours may be long or you may be feeling under the weather. Though the controversy continues, alternating between warnings of the sun's dangers due to high incidence of skin cancer and the obvious health benefits of natural sunlight, below is a list of only a few of the many known benefits of sunshine:

- By stimulating the synthesis of the "feel good" hormones, endorphins, chronic depression lessens, and our spirits lift.
- It stimulates the absorption of Vitamin D and its family of compounds that have been found to hinder cancer cell development.
- It jumpstarts our immune systems, helping to ward off illness.
- We sleep better at night through increased melatonin production.
- It increases calcium absorption and, thus, allows us to grow stronger bones, warding off osteoporosis. When Vitamin D is low, calcium absorption is hindered, and our bodies cannot absorb enough calcium to keep us in a state of optimum health, no matter how much calcium is added to the diet.

- Our cardiovascular system is improved through improved circulation.
- It relieves and reduces skin irritations.
- It can also help us lose weight by stimulation of our thyroid glands; this, in turn, stimulates our metabolic rate.

In days gone by, surgeons used sunlight to disinfect and heal wounds, but with the advent of antibiotics, sunlit hospital rooms and the hygienic and medicinal properties of sunlight have been left behind.

During my healing summer over twenty years ago, I often spent two-hour periods in the sun, until I found my way back to health. But that was then, and this is now. With the continual thinning of the ozone layer and skin cancer on the rise, caution should be used and, as always, a consultation with your doctor is best.

4. **BREATHING:** Oxygen is the body's most significant need, and breathing is the first thing we do when leaving the womb. The brain uses up to 20 percent of the body's oxygen supply, even though it occupies only 2 percent of the body's bulk. As we rush from place to place in our hurried lives, we may find ourselves taking very shallow breaths. When we tense our bodies, we have a tendency to practically stop breathing. Until our body forces that one long, deep breath to replenish itself, we may not even have been aware that our breathing was inhibited by stress. Deep breathing enriches and replenishes the oxygen in our lungs and

dispels the nitrogen that can build up and make one lethargic. It also has beneficial effects on our circulatory, nervous, and urinary systems, as well as skin and total body, mind, and spirit. When breathing deeply, we will find that we have more mental clarity, since the brain runs on oxygen.

If we can develop the habit of checking in with the body, becoming aware of ourselves, our breath or lack thereof, our thoughts, our thirst that we may not have quenched because we are too busy, our brains will function better, and our bodies will work more efficiently. When we can stop whatever it is we are doing to close our eyes, take a deep breath, and release it, we can rest in our breath, and that will allow our bodies to calm. When we keep our eyes closed and take a moment to actually listen to our bodies by employing our ears, this listening practice helps to bring us into the present moment.

By checking in, we are better able to get in touch with our body's needs and fulfill them *before* problems arise. We can appreciate the lighter moments better when we are tuned in, experiencing a moment of awareness.

Balance is essential when it comes to navigating through our lives, and paying attention to our breath allows us to develop self-awareness in the process. Through learning how to balance both the inside and the outside of our existence, we become fully awake and conscious of the Divine Presence that flows through every aspect of our lives. This enables us to experience life with joy, love, and a deep trust in the Universe.

5. **DIET:** In normal circumstances, nothing affects our body temple more than what we put into it. Our diet today has evolved far from the diet of our ancestors. Before the convenience of grocery stores, drive-thru take-outs, and packaged and processed foods, people were more prone to live in harmony with the foods found in their locale, derived from soil to mouth often without entailing the cooking process. Their diet consisted mostly of raw vegetables, fruits, grains, nuts and seeds. Much data is available on the healing properties of raw foods, and today there is a resurgence of interest in raw food diets. Many religions of the world advocate eating raw foods as a pathway to spiritual transcendence. Remember in my summer of meditation and healing I ate raw food exclusively. Watermelon and almonds were my staples, until toward the end other foods were minimally added.

Today, in our fast paced lives, well-rounded, timely, relaxed meals are becoming a thing of the past. Try to eat at approximately the same time each day, and if at all possible, avoid fast foods altogether by adding more vegetables, fruits and whole grains for proper nourishment. A good multi-vitamin also never hurts to fill in the gaps.

If blood sugar problems are a part of your daily existence, you may want to eat five smaller meals instead of the traditional three during the day. Be sure to include a source of protein with each meal as protein helps to stabilize blood sugar spikes, and I'm sure I don't need to tell you that sugar is a deal breaker.

Ingested sugar spikes the blood sugar level, and over a period of time, repeated spikes can result in diabetes. There are many other drawbacks and repercussions from eating sugar as well: It feeds cancer cells in the body; exacerbates depression, irritability, anxiety, mineral deficiencies, heart disease, and weight gain; and results in a suppressed immune system. Brain function is also impaired by too much sugar, and these are only some of the problems.

Here's a tip: If you crave sugar, eat something salty, like a dill pickle. This will dull your sweet tooth. Also, the best way to reduce your sugar intake is to buy fresh fruits and vegetables; the natural sugars in these wholesome foods will take the edge off of your cravings for unhealthy sweets and treats.

6. **MEDITATE:** Up to this point, I've spoken mostly about the spiritual benefits of meditation, but its medical benefits can range anywhere from weight loss to pain reduction to a more balanced personality. Meditation relieves stress and calms the mind. I shared in an earlier chapter that it was during meditation that I experienced a spontaneous remission when I was ill, and I truly believe in its healing power, because I've seen it firsthand in my own body.

Although there is much documentation on pain reduction related to meditation, one study in particular, published in *The Journal of Neuroscience*, reported that meditation "reduced pain intensity by 40 percent, in some people by up to 70 percent, compared with about 25 percent for morphine and other pain relievers." Even Dr. Fadel Zeidan, who led this pain reduction study, admitted that he was "surprised by the dramatic results" and "recommends practicing mindful meditation twenty to thirty minutes a day."

7. **WATER:** Sixty-four ounces of water daily will keep our systems properly hydrated. When our bodies become dehydrated by only 1 percent, we experience fatigue. Fluids such as coffee, tea, soda, lemonade, etc., are not the same as water; while they may be made with water, often the other ingredients in them work to dehydrate us as we drink them. Water should be taken into the body in its purest form, and although we may choose to consume other liquids, we shouldn't include those as part of our daily water recommendation.

In *The Body's Many Cries for Water*, Dr. F. Batmanghelidi actually recommends drinking half of our body weight in ounces of water each day, rather than the standard one-size-fits-all sixty-four ounces.

Dr. Batmanghelidi's story is interesting. He is originally from Iran, where he was spared execution with the masses when his captures discovered he was a medical doctor. He was thrown in prison to treat the ill and dying prisoners already in captivity, but they gave him no medicines or supplies with which to do so. The only "medicine" available to him was water, and he was amazed that the health of many patients actually improved by increasing their water intake. During his two-year incarceration, the doctor's prison literally became a test lab, and when he emerged a free man again, he wrote *The Body's Many Cries for Water,* so he could share the amazing stories of healing he had witnessed, with only water to fill the prescriptions.

The brain is the master organ of our body, and when it comes to water, the brain rules. The human body is comprised of over 60 percent water. When we're dehydrated, our minds become fuzzy, and we may find it hard to think clearly. When water is taken into the body, if a state of dehydration exists, the brain receives the water first. Until the brain is quenched, nothing else in the body becomes hydrated.

Drinking the proper amount of water each day may also enable one to lose weight, as it reduces fluid retention. By drinking two glasses of water thirty minutes before breakfast, lunch, and dinner, studies show that people have lost weight and kept it off. Appetite is reduced. With the intake of sixty-four ounces of water or more per day, the consumption of calorie-filled sodas and other drinks will typically be greatly reduced. Skin begins to glow, metabolism increases, and fat flushes from the body, also reducing cellulite. Water truly does appear to be a healing elixir.

8. **REST:** Sleep affects both our physical and mental wellbeing. Eight hours is optimum, but more may be required if one does hard physical labor during the day. This cessation of activity allows the body to rest and to repair and renew itself, as rest

encourages cell repair. Restorative, restful sleep also enables us to fight off colds and other viruses that attack the body, and it also improves brain function, giving us more mental clarity. Our skin takes on a healthy glow, and our eyes gain a sparkling radiance. These are some of the worthy benefits that bring us into an optimum state of wellbeing.

9. **EXERCISE:** From my own experiences, I know exercise is difficult when one is in need of healing or when we have experienced trauma. If you're not used to exercising and your illness, should you have one, doesn't preclude you, walking is the exercise I would recommend. During my healing summer, walking was one of the key ingredients that brought me back to health.

Just as our bodies need exercise, so do our brains. Exercise is an excellent aid for treating depression. Due to an increased secretion of the naturally produced chemicals serotonin and dopamine, our entire nervous system benefits from exercise. Tests have shown that in as few as ten minutes, exercise can also relieve stress and enhance our mood!

Risk of chronic diseases, such as diabetes and heart disease, are also reduced with walking. It's good for the heart and brings the body into a healthier state of alignment. Memory may also improve with the increased intake of oxygen. The bonus beyond these benefits and the others not mentioned here is that our self-esteem will generally improve.

Check with your physician first for his/her recommendations. If you're in a healthy state but are not used to exercising, and if your doctor recommends it, you may wish to begin with thirty minutes a day, four or five times a week. If you feel that's too much to start with, cut it back to three times per week at first, or cut the time down to fifteen or twenty minutes a day, remembering that some exercise is better than none, unless health issues are a consideration. The key to remember is that in order to benefit from any exercise program, we have to actually start one.

10. **VISUALIZATION:** To create a more positive setting for this, my recommendation would be to turn off the TV, turn on calming music, and read spiritual, self-help, or motivational books or articles. Remember, we are what we think, so we need to think positively about ourselves, our environment, our finances, our partner, our health, and our future. As we are co-creators in our lives, it is important that we shoot for the stars!

Dr. Joseph Dispenza, one of the most interviewed participants in the movie: What the Bleep Do We Know, and author of several books, including *Evolve Your Brain: The Science of Changing your Mind*, goes through a beautiful routine every morning: Before his feet touch the floor upon waking, he "creates his day." You may want to use it yourself. It's a practice of positive visualization, actually creating his own day, seeing it going perfectly throughout all the tasks set before him. Dr. Dispenza may be viewed discussing this practice at *www.YouTube.com/watch?v=G5nqMjPJhlA.*

Visualization helps keep your mind in order. For instance, you can utilize it when you're faced with stressful situations. Perhaps you have a big meeting or a difficult discussion with your partner, whatever your day holds; take a few minutes at the beginning of the day to see yourself in that meeting or conversation and see it going smoothly, with receptive listeners. Then see everyone in the room smiling in appreciation, or see your partner relaxed and attentive. When all is finished, feel the enthusiasm or the satisfaction of well-received, clear communication. Actually feel the pride and the pleasure within you that it's completed and you know that you were successful in your goal. Part of successful visualization is incorporating the actual feeling of what it would be like to achieve our goal. Employ the five senses as much as possible. If we can do this visualization beforehand, like a rehearsal, most things will go much more smoothly for us, and our chances of success will greatly increase.

In a test conducted among military marksmen, the shooters took aim and shot at their targets, as directed, then underwent a short period of visualization. They visualized themselves repeatedly hitting the center of the target, purposely felt that success, then shot again. At the end of the exercise, the accuracy scores soared above those that were completed without the visualization exercise.

The movie celebrity Jim Carrey has an amazing story about visualization, and how it helped him to achieve success. In 1987 Carrey wrote himself a check in the amount of 10 million dollars, but he dated the check "Thanksgiving 1995". His notation read: "For acting services rendered". Using visualization until his dream came to fruition, in 1994 he received a check for his role in Dumb and Dumber. The amount he received was 10 million dollars.

Other notables who credit creative visualization as one of the secrets of their success are: Oprah Winfrey, Tiger Woods, Bill Gates, Anthony Robbins and Will Smith to name only a few. Visualization exercises are powerful.

11. **AFFIRMATIONS:** Create new, positive thought forms through the power of affirmations. When you state your affirmation, stand in front of a mirror and look yourself straight in the eyes each morning upon rising and each evening before going to bed. Repeat these positive statements with meaning and conviction, while keeping your gaze on your reflection. Do this over and over for ten to twenty repetitions for every affirmation session.

It may feel strange or ridiculous at first, and it may be hard to imagine that merely saying these words will change the outcome; however, bear in mind that the more resistance you may feel toward the statement, the more often you should repeat it to yourself during the day as you perform your normal activities. In the evenings, use the mirror method again. It may take a few days for it to penetrate, but know that your words are being heard on a subconscious level. Like a record or CD, the more often you repeat it, the deeper the groove for change becomes.

Writing your affirmations in addition to repeating them out loud increases their effectiveness. This allows the brain to receive this information in two different ways: through the auditory system while reciting them, as well as through the visual senses when writing them. I caution you though, only do this practice if you are ready to see changes and improvements in your life!

You may want to create your own tailor-made affirmations, but below are a few samples to consider:

**HEALING**: "I am perfectly healthy in body, mind, and spirit. My (hearing, memory, pain...fill in the blank) is improving day by day."

**ABUNDANCE**: "I attract success and abundance into my life because that is who I am. Abundance and wisdom come to me daily from multiple sources."

**WEIGHT LOSS**: "I love my body and easily lose weight in a healthy way."

**WELLBEING**: "My life is in constant balance, filled with inner peace and joy. I now create my wonderful, ideal life. I love and accept myself exactly as I am. My life is good, rich, and beautiful."

Another affirmation that I use frequently, by Andrew Norvell from *Cosmic Magnetism* is: "I magnetize my...aura with the magnetic qualities of peace, goodness, truth, love and beauty, and these forces of attraction are in my personality."

12. **LAUGH:** The old adage, "Laugher is the best medicine," is not far from the truth. Laughter has been found to have many health benefits, including stress relief, increased energy, balancing the body, strengthening our immune system, and more.

Best of all, studies show that the same health benefits are derived, whether or not the smile or laugh is genuine. Thus, until one is able to truly enjoy a good, spontaneous belly laugh, we can practice and still receive the benefits. Watch funny movies, read funny books, and listen to good, positive comedians who tickle you into laughter.

People have healed themselves from the worst diseases by submerging themselves in laugh therapy. One of the most famous examples was Norman Cousins, a well-known, respected journalist who'd been given a death sentence. Suffering from a rare disease of the connective tissues and given only a few months to live, Norman sequestered himself in a hotel room, away from all negativity, including his doctors' gloom-and-doom prognosis, choosing a more holistic approach to healing with a new doctor of positive persuasion. His so-called "treatment" had depleted his body of Vitamin C, so he used massive doses of Vitamin C, along with humor and funny movies, and Mr. Cousins walked out of that den a healed man. Despite his previous constant pain, he had literally laughed himself well by staying in a positive environment and enjoying lots of big, deep belly laughs. He subsequently became known as "The Man Who Laughed Himself Back to Health," and instead of living only a few months, as forecasted by his doctors prior to his creative health regime, Norman Cousins went on to enjoy an additional twenty-six years of life!

You may have to force yourself to laugh at first, especially if you're in a difficult situation, but I encourage you to do so. There are so many benefits to laughter, and it is a habit that will help you enjoy better health and a longer, more joyful life. Not only that, but it's also contagious!

## MY JOURNEY TO HEALTHY EATING

Vegetarianism has a rich and varied background, tracing all the way back to ancient times. As an Essene, Jesus Himself was a vegetarian, and many religions advocate a vegetarian diet. The reason for this is because religions rely on and implement their sacred texts, which often do not mention meat as part of the diet. One theory is that by adhering to a vegetarian diet, spiritual enlightenment is more likely to be gained through a deeper connection with our Creator. Some also believe better health can be attributed to a vegetarian diet, and they don't believe in making animals suffer for their own nourishment.

When I first met Michael, I had not eaten meat for six years; I only ate what my body wanted me to eat: vegetables and fruits, legumes, and nuts. The vegetarian lifestyle was a process that evolved in a natural way for me. I loved hamburgers and could have eaten them morning, noon, and night. Then one day, the hamburger I was eating just didn't taste as good. Not too many weeks later, I felt a slight nausea coming on after lunch. I'd just eaten a hamburger. This progressed until I couldn't even hold a hamburger in my hand without having an unpleasant physical reaction. Next, it was roast beef. Even the smell of beef roasting in the oven sent me outdoors, in search of fresh air. As I live in the South, chicken-fried steak was next. At that point, I finally realized my body was trying to tell me something.

Bacon was extremely difficult for me to give up, but I'd made the choice to follow the will of my body. Me being me, it's as good as done when I've committed to something. I can't help myself, for that's who I am, whether I like it or not. Sometimes this trait doesn't always work to my advantage. Sometimes I don't see when it truly is time to occasionally give up on someone or something. But for the most part, my ability to commit has served me well.

I believe the change in my diet was one of the many reasons I was able to engage with the Holy Indweller as quickly as I did during my summer of healing. Through eating a more healthful, humane diet, my body was already vibrating at a higher frequency than it would have been had I still been following my old eating habits.

It's a choice we all have to make for ourselves, and it's a slippery slope when making the change. Emotionally, we may feel deprived at times; this may result in anger even though no one forced the decision upon us. When you try to take charge of your life, at first, the resistance and desire to continue your past choices may be strong. A nagging voice within may tell you that you deserve better, that it really doesn't make any difference if you make the change or not. For me, although I was able to go fairly comfortably without the meat I'd been raised on, it actually took a year before I stopped wanting bacon.

I made a pact with myself when I began changing my diet. I gave myself one year. I decided that if I went a whole year without eating bacon and still craved it at the end of that year, I'd make an exception and give myself permission to resume eating bacon! It was a challenge to forego bacon for a full 365 days, and toward the end of that year, I still wanted it. In my mind, I had accepted the fact that once I had hit the one-year mark, I would treat myself to bacon again. But a funny thing happened. Just a week before that one-year anniversary was up, the craving completely disappeared. The whole concept of eating bacon was a moot point, because suddenly, I didn't want any! Thinking back, I can only guess it was the Universe's way of testing my resolve up until the very last moment. This Universe of ours can be very mischievous.

Please know that I am not trying to convert anyone to vegetarianism. It's a road we have to travel ourselves in the decision-making process. I do what I do, but I don't expect everyone in the world to do the same. It's for each one of us to find what works best for our own bodies and for our own spirits. Sit quietly and think deeply upon this, and you'll no doubt find your own truth.

At first, there may be subtle pressure put upon those who make the switch. Well-meaning friends and families may joke about it. Certainly, when I gathered to dine with friends and relatives, everyone wondered and worried about what I "could" eat. At Thanksgiving, my mother would inevitably fret about it. Although there may have been ten things on the table other than the turkey, she was always afraid I would go hungry. If our feet are firmly planted on the path of healthy dietary changes, however, eventually others will come to accept it, and most will become very accommodating. They'll begin to worry less and less, knowing we can provide for ourselves and make our own decisions based upon what is available.

My first official date with Michael was an invitation to dinner. I assumed we were going to a restaurant, so I knew I'd be able to find something suitable on the menu. After he picked me up, I found out we were going to the home of two of his dearest friends. I didn't say anything, as I can usually always find delicious side dishes in any meal. As we drove through the countryside on our way to their house, with wide eyes, he suddenly turned to me and asked, "Do you eat meat?" I replied I didn't, "But I usually eat everything around it," I said.

As I recall, when we arrived, there was a big frenzy among our hosts, and my date because I didn't eat meat, and they were cooking steaks on the grill. Again, the familiar question voiced itself: "Um...are you going to be able to eat with us?" Everyone was worried about me, but as it turned out, I enjoyed a filling, healthy dinner of baked potato, salad, corn on the cob, and dessert!

When I stopped eating meat, I really didn't know anything about being a vegetarian, and I didn't bother to buy any books or do any research on the subject. I just made the changes on my own. In retrospect, it probably wasn't very intelligent, since I knew little about the importance of proper nutrition at the time, but I made the changes and educated myself along the way.

As I explained earlier, my body began to naturally evolve away from the meat sources I had previously enjoyed; that was my first acknowledgment, my first evidence that I needed to make the change. Although that was shortly before I began earnestly searching for my purpose in life, my inner guidance led me as it so often has, even while I was totally unaware.

After I'd stopped eating meat and began to educate myself, I discovered several important facts that supported my own personal decision and assured me that I had made the right decision for my own lifestyle. Although the figures used here have been updated, the premise remains the same.

Heart disease, obesity, and diabetes are all linked to consumption of saturated fats. Vegetarians consume fewer saturated fats and total fats than meat eaters. Mostly, there is a fear among the populace that if we give up meat in our diet, we won't consume enough protein; however, generally speaking, most Americans already ingest more protein than the body needs. Contrary to Western cooking, in other cultures, meat is used more as a condiment in dishes than as a main course. In this country, our meals are usually planned around the meat. Eating more meat, more protein, than the body needs can result in a number of problems and can adversely affect blood cholesterol levels.

Legumes are an excellent substitute for meat. These include pod-type foods with a row of seeds running along one side of them. Beans, lentils, and peas are excellent choices. Legumes contain less fat than meat, no cholesterol, and plenty of healthy minerals. They're also a good source of dietary fiber.

The Overseas Development Council estimates that annually, literally millions of pounds of grains that are now used to feed cattle could be freed for human consumption if Americans would simply cut their beef consumption by as little as 10 percent. Even if we chose not to cut meat consumption out completely, we would be taking that first step toward feeding the hungry in the world.

According to Dr. David Pimentel, in *Ecological Integrity: Integrating Environment, Conservation, and Health,* it takes an unbelievable average of about 12,000 gallons of water and 20 pounds of grain to produce just one pound of meat! In addition, as frightening as the thought may be, scientists agree that Earth may soon experience a water shortage. We can do our part to help alleviate or to forestall this looming water crisis by reducing our consumption of meat. It's a simple case of supply and demand. If we reduce our demand for food sources from the animal kingdom, the wise rancher will decrease the supply of animals accordingly. Planetary consumption would then be reduced, as there would be fewer animals in need of drinking water. Additionally, with fewer animals to graze, less water would be required to sustain their food sources of grains and grasses. The end result would be better water conservation in a time when our water supplies may be significantly challenged.

According to the July/August 2004 edition of *Crimes Unseen*, in an article by Dena Jones, in 2003, over ten billion animals were slaughtered for human consumption alone—ten billion with a B! The People's Ethical Treatment of Animals (PETA) organization estimates that the figure is nine billion, not ten billion, but they also add that millions more of these animals die from suffocation, stress, trampling, or lack of proper medical treatment.

Livestock raised en masse for meat are referred to as "factory-farm" animals. Most spend their lives in a disease-ridden, overcrowded, bleak existence. Calves are raised in cramped bins, so small that they cannot even turn around in their stalls. Chained to the sides of their prison, they can only move side to side their entire lives. These calves spend their short lives in these conditions just so we can enjoy a tender slice of veal.

The meat we buy in the supermarket has been processed. In other words, most of it has been slaughtered in the most inhumane ways, often after horrific transports. The USDA set out in Bulletin 589, page 1, later incorporated in the Revised Statutes of the United States, sections 4386 through 4390 inclusive, that no animal shall be transported more than twenty-eight hours without water, food and rest; but with unethical handlers, these periods can be longer, and sometimes in extremely high or low temperatures. From the time they are loaded into the trucks for transports to the slaughterhouses, their bodies are overcome with fear and stress, adrenalized as the victims stand, cluelessly awaiting their fate.

The fight-or-flight syndrome kicks in, but the cattle are captives, with no place to flee. The meat-packing industry is an industry indeed, and more money is made if more animals are killed. In a lackluster attempt at mercy, stun guns are used to stun the animals before the rest of the process takes place, but because the cattle are rushed through the shoots so quickly and workers are not always properly trained, the process often fails to alleviate the animal's sensitivity to the inevitable pain that follows. For many, without being first stunned, there is no sedation. The stress and fear hormones in the animals permeate their bodies, transferring from the blood into their tense muscles (meat). When the animal ultimately dies, the trauma vibration and hormonal residue remain in the meat; transferring like a toxin into our own body temples when that meat is consumed.

The chicken and poultry industry is no better. Beaks are routinely cut off without veterinarian assistance or anesthesia so the chickens don't peck each other while being overcrowded in cages that are far too small, and that is only one example of the cruelty and neglect and insensitivity that these animals go through before they are slaughtered. If you do choose to eat poultry, free-range chicken is, by far, the best way to go. Those birds are allowed the freedom to roam out of those small, overcrowded cages that most chickens are confined to for their entire lives. We become desensitized by picking up our neatly wrapped packages at the grocery stores, but the pain remains within, no matter how tidy it may appear on the outside. Surely these transgressions are not what the Universal Laws intended when Source gave us sustenance.

I remember my own transformation from eating the diet I had been raised on my whole life to allowing meat to fall from my food list. During the most difficult confrontation with myself, I stumbled upon the following quote from Nobel Peace Prize laureate, Issac Bashevis Singer. This premise quieted my ego's complaining arguments once and for all: "We are all God's creatures. That we pray to God for mercy and justice while we continue to eat the flesh of animals that are slaughtered on our account is not consistent."

If you choose to continue to eat meat, it would be beneficial to purchase it at your local health food store or natural market. Buy organic and free-range meat products whenever you can.

The last thing you need are more chemicals introduced into your body through the things you eat.

In the Islamic tradition, meat that is held to Islamic standards is called *halal,* and it is the Islamic equivalent of Kosher in the Jewish tradition. Both adhere to strict rules. Most health food stores today offer halal or kosher sections. Halal meat has only been killed in the most humane ways, and the fear toxins and chemicals that are added through traditional production and processing aren't present. For meat to carry the halal seal, certain criteria must be met:

- The animal must be raised in a humane, wholesome environment.
- It must not be caused discomfort during transport.
- It mustn't feel stress or fear before death.
- It must not be killed via continuous pain or injury.
- It must not be killed within view of other animals.

It's clear that none of these requirements are being met in today's factory-farm animal methods.

Our goal in proper nourishment is to raise the life force energy that vibrates throughout our bodies. In their most elemental forms, our bodies are comprised of energy. Every single part of us, as well as everything outside our bodies, can be broken down into energy, which can be defined as the indestructible base from which all life issues forth through vibration. This energy within the body vibrates at different levels, depending upon the fuel we put into it. Fruits and vegetables carry a much higher vibration than meat, and fruits carry the highest vibration of the food groups. Vegetables run a close second, and vegetables that grow above ground carry a higher vibration than those that grow below ground.

The more fruits and vegetables we consume and the more water we drink, the brighter and more open the seven energy centers (chakras) in our bodies become. The more dense the food we ingest, the more closed off these magical doorways of light become.

When we eat more fruits and vegetables and less meat, these chakras fill with life force energy. When this occurs, the energy centers open up even more as they become engorged, allowing them to shine more brightly. This becomes detectable in us from the outside as well, indicating outwardly how we feel inside. People may look at us in a curious way because we will shine more brightly from the higher vibration. Though others don't necessarily detect this particular light through their vision, their senses innately detect the improvement. On the outside, our eyes will brighten, our skin will radiate improved health, and our sense of calm will grow. As people enter our energy fields, compliments flow toward us. Andre Norvel, in *Cosmic Magnetism*, explains that cosmic magnetism is the "spark of life...the invisible cosmic beam of life energy that illumines your soul." Perhaps that's what people sense in us. As we develop a more positive personality and eat clean, fresh, chemical-free foods, people begin to gravitate toward us. In that improved state, on a soul level, others can innately sense this new, inner vitality.

After going through that summer of purifying and healthful eating, when I reentered the worldly space, I was often asked if I'd been working out. I looked and felt better than I'd ever looked or felt in my life. I could tell by their questioning looks and warm smiles that people sensed a positive change, even though they couldn't quite put their finger on it.

It's a given that alcohol, tobacco and drugs are not good for us, but on the spiritual path, ingesting meat, sugar, and caffeine are also detrimental when we are striving to quiet the mind and raise our level of vibration for meditation. This is not to say you won't receive benefits from meditating if you ingest these; I am simply stating that it is a more arduous route. Vegetarianism and healthful consumption accelerate the process of quieting the mind, but that's not the only path that leads to gnosis. Even if you don't choose to change your diet, don't give up on meditation. We all have free choice, and I am simply pointing out what works better for most, myself included.

**CHAKRAS**

Since I mentioned our energy centers in the foregoing section, I would like to briefly clarify this for those who may not be familiar with this concept. *Chakra,* literally translated as "wheel," comes from the language of ancient Sanskrit. Sometimes chakras are referred to as "the wheels of life," as they stir the life force energy throughout our physical bodies like tiny fans. In esoteric teachings, we learn that these wheels are spinning constantly inside our bodies, constantly radiating and receiving energy. It may be easier to think about them as energy centers; like large cities require power plants to generate energy, these centers are the power plants of our bodies.

These chakra wheels spin at different rates of speed, depending upon what is happening in our lives and where they're located in our bodies. Each chakra is also represented by a specific color linked to its location. The lower chakras spin more slowly than those in higher locations, and there are many of them in our bodies. Some religious texts say there are as many as 88,000 of them, but below are the 7 to which most references are made.

To further explain, I ask that you visualize your spine. These wheels of life are spaced periodically along the spinal column, beginning with the Root Chakra located in the base of our spines. This energy center is represented by the color red. The red chakra is affected by our thoughts and feelings concerning our safety and security. It's also the sexual center for the male.

Above the Root Chakra is the Sacral Chakra, about two inches below your navel. The Sacral Chakra corresponds to the color orange and concerns such things as self-image, weight, sleep patterns, cravings, risk-taking, compulsive behaviors, creativity, and emotions, including feelings of self-worth. It's also the sexual center for the female.

As we continue to travel up from the base of the spine, we reach the chakra of the solar plexus. It's located approximately two inches below your breastbone. It spins in accordance with our feelings of power or powerlessness and control or lack of control in our lives. Yellow signifies the Solar Plexus Chakra.

The Heart Chakra begins the higher-vibrating chakras and is located in the middle of the chest, behind the breastbone. It's represented by the color green and is concerned with our thoughts and feelings regarding every single one of our relationships in life. The Heart Chakra is the center for outgoing and incoming love and our ability to love or be loved. This is the chakra that ties body, mind, and spirit together.

Above the Heart Chakra is the blue Throat Chakra, located at the Adam's apple. Appropriately, the Throat Chakra is affected by our thoughts and feelings regarding our ability or inability to communicate in all of our relationships in life, even those with our Source of Creation.

The sixth chakra is our Third Eye Chakra, sometimes called the Brow Chakra because it's located above the eyes, in the center of our forehead. It's represented by the color purple. Our ability to receive spiritual guidance and tune in to our higher self is located in this powerful energy center, and this is where psychic ability resides.

Finally, the Crown Chakra, the highest of all energy centers, is located at the top of the head. The Crown Chakra is our spirituality center and vibrates faster than any of the other chakras. Through the Crown Chakra, we receive enlightenment, direct connection with the Divine; this is our cosmic consciousness. White and purple are the primary colors of the Crown Chakra, giving it a beautiful violet hue.

Often when we're feeling ill, sluggish, irritable, or negative, it is because our chakras are blocked with stagnant, dark energy that suppresses their beautiful hues of color. Our diet can affect the transference of life energy found in these centers; so also can our positive or negative attitudes.

I refer back to the energy work my friend practiced on me when I was ill during my healing summer. That work afforded my energy centers the necessary clearing to bring them back to their radiant alignment so my body could begin its overall journey to health. The body cannot begin to heal itself until the electrical circuits are brought back into balance. Through the energy worker, my energy centers were cleansed, and the doors that were holding back clogged energy were opened, allowing me to return to a state of healing and wellbeing. If you don't have access to energy practitioners, there is a way to clear the chakras without incurring any expense. Have I mentioned meditation before?

*"Within your physical form is a secret door to divinity. Hasten your evolution by proper diet, healthful living, and reverence for your body as a temple of God. Unlock its sacred spinal door by the practice of scientific meditation."*
**Paramahansa Yogananda**

## ENTRAINMENT AND THE HEART

Physics explains entrainment as two vibrating objects that vibrate at different speeds when separated but eventually begin to vibrate at the same speed when brought into close proximity to each other. Mysteriously, they become in sync with each other without outside interference when one object slows and the second object increases its speed through the exchange of small amounts of energy that are transferred between the two objects. This has also been the case in small offices, where women work in close proximity of one another; it is not mere urban legend that over a period of time, their menstrual cycles will align.

The mystery of entrainment is this: If you put two pendulum clocks together within close proximity of each other, with their pendulums initially going in different directions, after a period of time, the clocks will eventually come into rhythm with each other, and you'll eventually find that the pendulums will swing in the same direction all by themselves, without any outside interference. This is a simple example of entrainment.

In my previous chapter on "Empathic Childhood," I shared a story about wanting to put the two soup cans together so they wouldn't be alone and would become friends. It was fuzzy to my thinking as a child, but somehow, even at that tender age I knew there would be some connection between two like objects when they were kept in close proximity to one another over a period of time. Earlier, I mentioned that everything vibrates with energy.

Through my intuition, even though I was unaware of entrainment as a term or definition, I knew that something would eventually cause the cans to begin vibrating at the same frequency. In my childlike mind, the vibration of two like objects that came into resonance with each other, within close proximity of each other, translated into friendship, and to me at that age, those cans would have then been the best of friends.

In my own experience with the power of entrainment, in preparation for meditation one day, I decided to connect with my guide, Shakh Muhammad Said al-Jamal ar-Rifa'I, more fondly referred to as Sidi. Though he was in Jerusalem at the time, I had learned an entrainment process while studying Sufism. I went over to his picture on my bookshelf and picked up his photo, then stared into his eyes. I had learned in teachings from both my guide and my guru that if you stare for a period of time into the eyes of the one you wish to connect with, without blinking, the connection will be made. There are a number of ways this could play out. Perhaps that person will think of you at that particular moment or even call you. You may even run into them unexpectedly, or they may begin speaking to someone else about you.

Though Sidi was far away at the time, in Jerusalem, as I held the picture and stared into his eyes for a few minutes, Sidi's eyes began to open wider, then suddenly began to open and close, open and close, open and close incredibly quickly—so fast that I wondered if he could possibly have blinked that quickly in real time. They continued to do that until I looked away. I was astonished. I completed a deep meditation and felt so connected with the result that the entrainment exercise and the meditation had produced that I was guided to read from his writings. When I randomly opened *Music of the Soul*, my eyes fell upon these words: "I am with you always. No matter how far the distance between us, I see you." This verified to me, beyond a doubt, his omnipresence.

It's now thought that a mother's heart function may also be a pattern set for her own baby's heart education as the baby lies against the mother's beating chest. Through entrainment, a blueprint may stencil itself upon the baby's heart, transferring from the mother's heart through energy exchanges and electromagnetic waves, as though the two hearts were in telepathic communication. This could further explain the bonding effect between mother and child, perhaps even in our relationships with our partners. When our hearts are in close proximity of each other over a period of time, entrainment could explain why our hearts are said to "beat as one."

There is an extraordinary experiment discussed in *The Biology of Transcendence* by Joseph Chilton Pearce. Mr. Pearce and his fellow researchers conducted laboratory experiments on the hearts of rodents. When they removed one heart cell and put it under a microscope for investigation, they observed that it remained stable for a short time, then began to beat erratically before it eventually died. When two heart cells were removed and studied independently, they also suffered the same consequences. Only when they varied this did they witness the magic of entrainment. Two heart cells were removed and, as before, began to beat erratically before they died. However, before death overtook each one of them, when placed within close proximity of each other, each heart cell stabilized, regained strength and rhythm, and began beating in sync, independent even of the heart from which they had come! This was true even when a partition was placed between them, provided they remained within close proximity of each other.

This is one provocative thought I've been mulling over: I'm certainly no scientist, but this thought has occurred to me more than once. As the very basis of the Universe and all things in it is energy, the birthing of all that we know must come from yet a higher energy vibration (source). When speaking of the human phenomena of entrainment, according to Stephen Rechtscheffen in *Timeshifting,* it is "our unconscious drive to get in step with the dominant rhythm." This could explain the deep calling within that so many of us experience. Perhaps the entrainment process is the very vehicle through which our Creator brings us into sync with Him/Her, the highest vibrating energy in existence. It is my belief that through entrainment, the Immortal Shelter is ever beckoning us back to Him. To use the words "dominant rythm" of Rechtscheffen again, what could have a more "dominant rhythm" than God Almighty, the Creator of all?"

The heart produces the strongest, largest electromagnet field of all the organs in the body, even more prominent than the brain. Research indicates that this electromagnetic field is shaped like a large donut, with our bodies in the hole. The heart emanates in a constantly shifting energy, traveling outward in a living arc, then curving down along the sides in a rounded formation, returning to the source (heart) in the same manner as in the shape of a donut. Research shows that this electromagnetic arc extends, more or less, the full length of the body, from the bottom of the pelvis to the crown of the skull, and that it extends all around us, outward to a distance of twelve to fifteen feet, with the first three feet emanating the strongest signals.

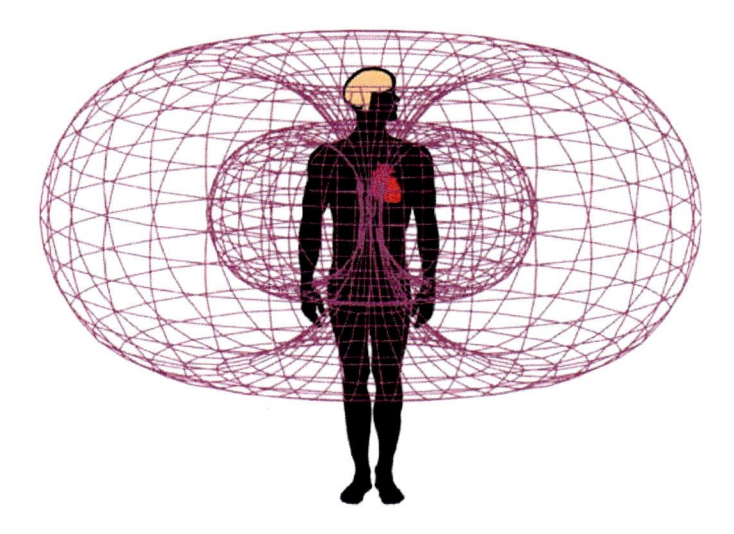

Copyright © Institute of HeartMath Research Center

In our relationships then, as we stop to speak to a friend or give a dollar to a stranger, the torus (or donut) of our hearts overlaps with each other. Like a holographic pattern, we are able to read each other's energy on a subconscious level while our arcs are overlapping, giving and receiving information simultaneously.

Previously, I gave an example of how others may be drawn to us for some seemingly inexplicable reason. The cleaner, more pure our bodies and minds are, the more our heart resonates with the universal Source. We exert these electromagnetic fields much like metal filings react when a magnet is placed beside them. Thus, some people are said to have a magnetic personality that draws us to them.

When a magnet is placed above metal filings, the individual shards of metal are then drawn upward to the magnet, until they are actually lifted up from the surface and adhere to the bottom of the magnet above them. Perhaps this is a perfect metaphor for our own life experience and the transformative experience of death, when we are drawn back to our Source.

If the whole Universe emanates as a giant torus, as it is now believed by scientists, and everything in creation also has its own individual torus, which it is now believed, then we, as humans, may be like metal filings, constantly being drawn back to our Creator, the greatest Magnet of them all!

Again, this may explain why we feel a calling, an inner need for something more, a spiritual void when we're not connected to Source, a need to search for our purpose or completion in our lives. Until we return to our Creator through the most transformative experience, it only makes sense to make all of our relationships loving ones, in preparation for the gift that is to come.

## SIMPLICITY

The laws of life are unchanging, even in our constantly changing world. They are timeless and forever. It's up to each of us to seek out these higher laws and to live by their credo in order to advance the soul's evolution. The Ten Commandments are certainly a great start, but what of those who came before Christianity, before those stone tablets meant to guide us to a better way of living?

Periodically throughout history, greatly enlightened souls have incarnated to lead the mass of humanity back to the spiritual laws of life through revelations received from the Highest Source.

In our American way of living today, accumulation seems to be the thought that preoccupies our minds: *How can I get a bigger house, a newer car, and a better job so I'll have more money to buy more, bigger, and better things?*

One of the great laws of life is simplicity, which was the core of many of Jesus' teachings. This is the law from which our culture has deviated and continues to do so, perhaps more than any other throughout history. When we have what we need, we are safe. When we have what we want, we are often buried in a world of clutter and excess. We're searching for something to fill the hole inside of us, but more material objects will not suffice. We'll become bored and will want to move on to the next new thing and then the next, keeping us on a wheel, like a hamster exerting all this energy but going nowhere. We lead lives of diversion and distraction, looking onward and outward instead of inward and upward.

Self-esteem can only be born from the inside out, not the other way around. We don't need to *show* others our worth by having a bigger home or a more expensive car or more toys than our acquaintances. The thirst we are trying to quench is a thirst for a Godly connection. When we find this, excess becomes unnecessary.

Advanced teachers periodically come to mankind to guide us back to our main course. The practice of simplicity in our lives allows us to turn our attention from earthly entrapments, back to our Heavenly Father, our greatest Provider. When our homes and lives are de-cluttered from the excess we have accumulated, our minds become clean, free of the reflection of the disorder mirrored in our outside environment. When our minds become clean, we no longer trip over the rubble that once blocked our path, and our attention will turn inward in our search for what really matters in our lives. Ultimately, if we continue to peel the onion down to the heart, we find that what really matters are the answers to these ultimate questions: Why are we here? And where are we going?

> *"Simplicity, clarity, singleness...these are the attributes*
> *that give our lives power."*
> **Richard Holloway**

**ASK FOR HELP**

In their creation, the All set aside for mankind one gift He didn't bestow upon His angels. Man has free will, but angels were created only to do God's will. Sometimes, that gift of free choice can get us into trouble, and consequences are inevitable when we make the wrong decisions. When these woes befall us, it helps us to know that there are legions of angels standing by, waiting to help. Invite them, for they want to be asked. They want to assist us. They are all around us, waiting to do God's bidding.

Our challenge, when times get tough or fear overcomes us, is to remember that we're not alone. Help is readily available to us if we only ask and allow the angels to come to our rescue. If you don't feel that assistance is there, just ask for it with an open heart. Then, when the help does come, don't write it off as mere coincidence. If doubts still remain with you after your predicament has been solved or after your fear has subsided, I invite you to try asking again and again in other situations until the foundation of your belief system has been set. This allows us to let go of our notion of coincidence. Fortunately for us, the Divine is generous with our chances to know Him.

I'm very blessed to have Sara Hickman as a good friend. She is also an incredible musician and songwriter, based in Austin, Texas. She is beloved by the world, and her songs are beautiful and inspiring, so good that many famous musicians have recorded those precious lyrics penned from her hand.

Sara has been doing service work through her music since she was seven years old, and she is constantly involved in more than one service project at a time, donating her time and talents. She often comes up with these service opportunities in her own beautiful mind, because she is the type of person who looks around, sees something in our society that needs to be fixed, and sets in motion programs that can lend a hand. She is amazingly talented and has previously held the title of State Musician of Texas. On top of that, she is one of the most devoted mothers I know and has a beautiful family.

I mention Sara because she can personally attest to the miraculous things that can result when the principles in this book are followed. This example, a story of seemingly bad things happening to good people, happened just recently.

On several occasions, we've had the joy of watching Sara's family pet, Lucky, when she and her family must travel. During the most recent occasion, I called Sara, as I'd forgotten to share with her that I thought Lucky might have an ear infection. When she answered the phone, her voice was different than I'd ever heard it. After more conversation, she broke down and poured her heart out, telling me that she was at her breaking point, facing four huge challenges simultaneously in her life. To make matters worse, her father had just recently passed away, and her heart was still raw with grief.

She was also disappointed. Willie Nelson was set to record

a song she'd written, but Mr. Nelson and the law had just had a misunderstanding, and she was sure he would no longer be able to do the recording for her. She was particularly troubled about that turn of events, as she had committed to donate all of the proceeds from the CD to an organization called Theater Action Project (TAP). TAP was relying heavily on that forthcoming donation to help its cause: to bring the arts to children in schools where funding has been cut.

While listening to Sara, I realized I couldn't solve these problems for her. I couldn't personally change or move the mountain of trials she was facing. I could only offer the sympathy and empathy that welled up inside me, and I knew she needed someone who could do more. We talked at length on the phone that day, and from my own experiences, knowing the expediency with which this practice works, I suggested that she get down on her knees and pour out all of those feelings from the deepest depths of her soul and implore the Immortal Listener for help. Then we hung up.

The following is an e-mail I received from her within a couple hours after our visit together:

> I was on my knees, crying and praying, asking God so many things, thanking God for loving me and for knowing what I wanted to say, even though I was crying so hard and couldn't find the words. Then I took Lili to the store (she doesn't feel well, as you know, but matzah ball

> soup always helps), and I came home, and one problem was done. Willie Nelson recorded my song yesterday! Thank you, Ginger. Bless you. I love you through this sorrow and fire I am in!

In the Sufi tradition, trials are referred to as being in the fire, and joys are referred to as being in the garden. I had shared this with Sara as we commiserated in our phone conversation, so she made ready reference to it in her e-mail.

It gave me great joy to share with her my tried and true solution that has worked for me in the past, without fail. When we feel we are going under for the third time, as though we are about to become a drowning victim in the flood of our trials, God hears our pleas and responds. As you can likely tell from her e-mail, her words and plea came from the depths of her soul. As the Universe hears our heartfelt intentions, it will often spring to our rescue, even when words are absent. The language of sincerity and surrender is strong.

*"Never think God does not answer your prayers.*
*Every word you have whispered to Him is written*
*in His heart, and someday He will answer you."*
**Paramahansa Yogananda**

# CHAPTER 9

## My Validations

**LIFE'S STAIRCASE**

When you pray, don't pray with your heart half-open. Your Father created you! There's no one like you! He is there for you, to hear your sorrows, your troubles, and your desires. He knows you are perfect, just the way you are. He doesn't care if you're cleaned up or ragged, rich or poor, man or woman. All He desires is that you return His love.

Remember, sometimes it may be in our best interest when our requests are *not* met. We're merely human, after all, and often we can't see the larger picture or the greater opportunity that looms ahead for us. Perhaps we don't get that job we thought would be perfect for us, but then we are offered a better job in its place, one we never would have known about had our prayer for the original position been answered the way we wanted.

It's important to know that should your prayer not materialize on the spot, you *will* still get an answer, as long as your intentions are pure and your belief is strong. Patience is the key, along with recognizing that the prayer may not be answered in the exact way you are expecting. Perhaps when we feel our prayers are unanswered the unspoken response may be "Wait" or "I have something better."

It may take some time to recognize that a prayer has been answered, and without reflection, we may feel that our prayer was not answered at all. We may not see the big picture as our Creator does. In many cases, He has something better in mind for us than we have for ourselves. If we surrender to this truth and take the time to sit back and reflect, we may see that our prayers have been answered in a way we never expected. Be open and trust that your words are heard. The Universe wants to give to us whatever it is that we want, provided that it is for our highest good. Have patience and trust, patience and trust.

In the third grade, I thought one of my prayers had gone unanswered. When my mother and father separated, I wore out my knees, praying and pleading at night, "Please, God, let Mommy and Daddy get back together again." I must have repeated that prayer a thousand times or more. Ultimately, my parents opted for divorce, though they did remain on friendly terms.

Within a few years, my mother remarried, and so did my father. Many years passed, and my stepfather had a fatal heart attack. The status of my father's marriage was on shaky ground, and another divorce was on the horizon for him. More years passed, and my mother, still single, relocated to another state. Not long afterward however, she returned, and she and my father were together from that time forward, until she made her transition years later. That prayer wasn't unanswered at all! Over twenty years had passed since I had prayed so hard for their reunion, but ultimately, I came to realize our prayers *are* answered, but always in God's time, not necessarily on our own time schedule.

One problem we have in realizing that our prayers have been answered is remembering what we asked for in the first place. Many times, we ask God for one thing or another, and because it doesn't happen within *our* allotted time period, we forget we ever asked. We simply move on to the next thing and the next, until our previous desires are left in the ever-receding, dim past.

In the big plan of life, our individual lives cannot be worked on a schedule, no matter how much we would like it that way. We are put through learning experiences when we are ready for them and not until. The proper way to walk up a staircase is one step at a time, and each step is slightly farther back from the front than the one before it. They stack, as do our experiences for our learning and growth. So many times, I've experienced something, only to forget all about it. At some point in the future, I am usually reminded of that experience, and only then am I able to discern how that prior experience might have been a teaching step for me, one that enables me to make a wiser choice in a current situation.

Time sometimes passes before we receive what we wanted

long ago. When this happens, we may take credit for it ourselves or feel we are just lucky, or perhaps we don't even reflect on it at all. We just move in the flow of life and take the next thing that comes to us. Take me for example, my friend married a wealthy young man, and they moved to a new, very elite neighborhood with a country club and rolling green hills and an abundance of trees. Their home was secluded behind high shrubbery, down a steep hill from the street. In my early adulthood, I visited that friend, in total wonderment that at our age, she was already living in such a fine home. I asked silently that I would be able to live in that neighborhood one day.

As time went by, they moved to another state, and we lost contact. Years later, by the grace of God, I met and married the man of my dreams, and we lived in a few different homes throughout the years. Our current home is in a wonderful neighborhood, although it is not one of the newer areas in town.

Once, on my way to run some errands, I noticed that some shrubs and greenery were being cleared alongside the road in our neighborhood. When I looked down the steep slope, I was surprised to see my friend's secluded house from years ago. I had totally forgotten she had lived in that vicinity, but there was that house I had admired all those years before, now partially exposed to street view due to the cutting of the hedges. The prayer I had muttered in my early adulthood came back to me with crystal clarity; my "one day" had arrived. I had been living for almost two years in the same neighborhood I had asked to live in so many years ago, but I'd forgotten to thank God for his excellent memory.

Our prayers *are* answered. When we take the time to quiet the outer world through prayer, we tap that inner wisdom that never disconnects from the Almighty. That wisdom is so deep, so real that it cannot and will not fail us.

**SOUL LANGUAGE**

When we tap into our inner wisdom, which encompasses knowing, conscience, intuition, and guidance, we should recognize that each of these is a gift from God, readily available when we become acquainted with our true self. Inner wisdom is the language in which the soul communicates with us. Knowing, conscious, intuition, and guidance are all deeply intertwined, with only subtle differences.

**KNOWING** is simply the truth unveiled; it is certainty beyond doubt. This is when the soul is talking to us from the deepest depths of our core of existence. As man was given the gift of free choice, we may choose to follow the advice, or we may not. When we follow that directive, the right life choices are made. These right choices save us pain and suffering, or at least greatly reduce them, even if pain and suffering are what we need to go through to learn our life lesson. Earlier, I shared that I told my mother it was my knowing telling me that if I married Michael, we would have a happy marriage. Knowing always comes from within.

**CONSCIENCE** stems from the Universal. It was created to keep us in alignment with the principles that guide us to our higher good; this, in turn, leads us on our road to evolution. It is another thread in the tapestry of knowing. The Laws of the Universe delineate between right and wrong. When we cross from the boundary of good action and are in touch with our true selves, we receive an internal indication that we've gone out of bounds. We can then correct our course through an apology and a good act toward those whom we have wronged. In some cases, though, more amends may be required. Our conscience will always let us know when we have done enough. The right action steers us back on course to good works, and our conscience is usually appeased through righting the wrong or by continuing to right it. When conscience is repeatedly ignored, it becomes debilitated under layers of disregard that may build up to shield it, and then the voice of conscience is no longer heard until we arrive at some form of reconciliation.

The conscience usually kicks in before we've even committed the act or uttered the words we're contemplating. Through a sort of well-meaning nagging, it often gives advance warning of the regret we are about to create and the wounds we may incur, but emotions may push this warning aside. As we all have free choice, it is up to each of us as individuals to choose the high road when we are given the chance.

**INTUITION** is a branch on the tree of truth. It may give us a preview of truth through a feeling. Intuition can be compared to looking behind a façade. It may be a hunch or a nudge in one direction or another. It can come as a warning of lurking danger or in a particular way of thinking, such as whether a person is trustworthy or not. It can also give us direction in taking one choice of action over another choice of action. Intuition by some is written off as common sense, but common sense comes from drawing upon past experiences that have served as education. Beyond our everyday consciousness lies intuition.

When we find ourselves at an unclear road sign, a crossroads in our travels that forces us to make a choice in which direction to proceed, we usually sit there for a few minutes as we try to make the right decision. This allows our intuition to guide us, as long as we remain in a calm state, actively listening to our internal readings. We may detect a nudge in one direction over another. It's usually when we don't take the time, when we become frustrated, shutting out intuition and blindly jerking the steering wheel in one direction or the other in frustration, that we end up at a dead end. This road sign example could refer to a specific situation or a metaphor for life in general. Intuition offers less clarity than knowing, but the feeling of direction is there just the same. Intuition and knowing both come from within.

The advice given earlier about remembering to ask for help also applies here. By sitting in quietude and taking the time to ask in which direction we should turn at that confusing road sign or moment in life, then by exercising patience and taking time to listen for the answer to our question, our chances of having a more successful journey will be greatly increased.

**GUIDANCE** is also different from knowing. While knowing is being sure beyond a shadow of a doubt, it always comes from within. Guidance, on the other hand, may come from within us or outside of us.

Earlier, I spoke about our motor home trip, when I failed to share my guidance with Michael when we were traveling and the tire suddenly blew out. My silence in that situation endangered us both. My guidance was simple: "Hold on!" It was received from an outside Source but came to me from inside my head as a telepathic voice. Visitations by Heavenly Beings bring outer guidance, as do signs, if we pay close attention to them when they appear to us. In knowing, we simply know. In guidance, there are times when we don't.

Though I wasn't there to see it, my great-grandmother had an experience when she was young, and the story has trickled down through the annals of my family history. There may be times when we are metaphorically lost in the fog but intuitively know what we need to do to get back on course. Then again, there may be times we are literally lost in the fog, and we need an outward sign to guide us in the right direction.

My great-grandmother experienced the latter when she was a small child. She wandered too far out into nature without supervision. A dense fog rolled in, and she became lost, unable to discern which direction she should go to return to safety. As she stumbled along, not knowing in which direction to turn, she saw a white lamb standing off to one side. It was barely visible, as it was almost the same color as the swirling blanket that enveloped them both.

Anxious to pet the woolly creature, she forgot about her plight and changed her course. As she approached it, she reached out, but the lamb took a few cautious steps back. As she moved forward to try again, the lamb stepped back even farther. This cycle continued until, as quickly as the fog had come, it began to clear. When she heard her family call her name, she turned but for a moment to look in their direction, and when she turned again to look at the lamb, it was gone.

Looking around for the lamb in all directions, she stood there as the family ran to her. Nearby was a sheer cliff. Her family owned a large cattle ranch in a fairly isolated area, with no sheep. Even after checking beyond the embankment, the small lamb she had tried to pet was nowhere to be seen. The only feasible explanation was that God had intervened and sent an angel in the form of a lamb to guide my great-grandmother to safety, away from the edge of the cliff. This is a perfect example of external guidance, and a sweet story to tell.

Now, I'd like to share more stories with you, personal validations that have affirmed my faith that help is ever present in the unseen world.

## LOCKED OUT

A few years ago, Michael had to go out of town for work. We had just moved into our new neighborhood, and I had not yet met any of the neighbors. It was almost midnight, and I was ready for bed, other than letting my three dogs out briefly before we turned in for a good night's sleep. I was barefoot and in my nightgown as I opened the back door and waited for them to return from the yard. Since it took longer than I expected, I took a few steps out onto the patio to urge them to hurry up. As I stood peering into the darkness beyond the porch light, I heard the back door close softly behind me, due to a draft. The dogs ran up happily behind me, and when I turned to open the door, I found that it was locked.

The front door was already locked, as I was preparing to go to bed, but I didn't panic because I remembered that a spare key was hidden in the front yard. I walked around the front of the house in my bare feet to retrieve the key, only to find several teenage boys parked across the street, standing around their cars. I had to move about stealthily in my nightgown, as our front floodlights were on to light our drive. Once I had the key in hand, I opened the front door and slipped inside. Not wanting to put the key back with the boys outside, I put it on the floor in front of the door so I'd remember to replace it first thing in the morning. Next, I went to the back door again to let the dogs back in so we could all go to sleep, but they weren't there anymore, and I couldn't see them. I could only assume they'd gone to the front area of the side yard when I had gone out the gate. I was frustrated as it was almost midnight, and I didn't want to call out for them and wake everybody in the neighborhood, so I decided to lean out just a little farther to call to them in a whispery voice I was sure only they would hear. Just as I did so, I heard the door *click* again behind me.

*Ugh*! Now the extra key was locked inside, and I was locked out, for the second time that night. My dogs ran back to me as though it was good news. I was outside with no shoes, with no spare key and no cell phone to call for help, no husband at home to come to my rescue and I was wearing nothing but my nightgown. I didn't know any of my neighbors, and even if I had, I wouldn't have wanted to wake them at that hour.

I decided I had no other option but to rescue myself. I walked around the house and tried the doors and all the windows for a second time, only to find them locked. As the side door to the garage was within our gated and locked backyard fence, we usually left the garage door unlocked. In the unlocked garage, I could retrieve a hammer. My plan was to break a window and let myself inside the house.

In retrospect, the window that I chose would not have been the wisest choice, but at the time, I thought it would work. I only needed a ladder. Still in my nightgown, I pulled the ladder from the garage and climbed it, then drew back the hammer to tap the glass. Just before I swung, the thought struck me: *I haven't even asked for help! I'm trying to do this all on my own. I haven't included my Greatest Protector in this plan at all!*

Standing on the ladder, I uttered a prayer for aid and assistance. As I finished that prayer, I looked up at the sky. The moon was beautiful beyond words, almost full and the whitest white I'd ever seen. I had not even noticed it before. Overwhelmed with gratitude for the beauty we so often overlook, tears filled my eyes as I lowered my head and the hammer. I forgot about the locked door and the window as I gave thanks for the gift of that night.

Just as I did so, a mighty breeze came out of nowhere. It was so strong that I had to hold on to the bottom of the window ledge to keep from blowing off the ladder. I sensed it had come from around the corner, from the front of the house, as it was blowing straight down the side of the house to where I stood. The only issue was that to do that, it would have to make a forty-five-degree turn. I had the strong sense that *something* or *someone* was arriving. The wind was strong enough that my long hair was blowing away from my face, almost straight out behind me, and my gown was pressed against my body, lapping at the back of my legs. Nevertheless, as I stood in the great rush of wind, my awareness fell on a small branch just inches from my head,. It was standing in still attention, without as much as a quiver. Not one rustle from the leaves of the trees in my vicinity escaped into the night. The night around me, except in my tunnel of wind, seemed absolutely quiet; no breeze was disturbing anything at all!

Just as the realization shot through me, I recognized the telepathic male voice that had come to my assistance in the past. Inside my head, I heard the firm request: "Try again." I checked all the windows and doors in the back for the third time. As I went around to the front of the house to do the same, I realized I had not yet checked the wood and glass double-doors that led into our cozy living room in our office. That door was always kept locked, so I hadn't felt compelled to check it. Without rechecking anything else, I walked straight to the office. Knowing the door would open before I turned the knob, I gave thanks and walked into our house for a good night's rest.

About a year after I received that blessing, without having shared the story above, I was sitting in one of my classes, and the teacher was speaking on the topic of angels. He explained that one way to tell when angels are present is that a breeze often accompanies them. "This breeze," he said, "may be as subtle as an air-conditioning cycle turning on or the rustling of leaves on a tree." In that instant, I remembered the great rush of wind that seemed to come from along the front of the house and somehow turn a sharp angle. That day, I learned that the mighty breeze I felt that evening was one of the trademark signs that angels had come to help me.

**BUZZARDS**

Michael and I are fortunate to be able to split our time between our home in town and our ranch, a little over one hour away. On one occasion when we were going to spend the weekend in the country, we had to take two cars because our schedules didn't match up. Michael left about thirty minutes before me. As I drove the scenic route, my phone rang. It was Michael, asking how soon I could be there. He told me that one of our horses was down, and he'd already called the veterinarian. Not knowing if it would survive or not, I sped on.

As I topped a steep hill near our property, I glanced out in the distance to see a huge swirl of black buzzards circling above our property, over the area where our barn was. There were so many of the feathered scavengers that they formed a wide, black circle, sailing lazily in one large mass on the thermals. I was amazed that they could know so quickly that there might be trouble.

I glanced quickly back at the road for two or three seconds to see if I needed to make any corrections. As I glanced back up to watch them again, the cloudless blue sky was completely empty. I was coming down a long hill, and visibility was covered at a 180-degree angle. The birds had been in the sky in front of my car less than a quarter-mile away. Now, there was not one bird in sight, none swirling, leaving, or otherwise.

I had no idea how so many birds could have disappeared so quickly without a trace. From that hill, I could see for miles to the right and left, even a panoramic view of the sky ahead. I wondered about that odd phenomenon as I entered the gate and drove directly to the barn. The veterinarian pulled in right behind me, and a short time later our trusty, beautiful friend was put to rest.

My dear husband had seen nothing, even though both man and ailing horse were outside the barn. The only explanation I have is that, in His benevolent grace, I was given that vision to prepare me for what was ahead.

**ART CLASS**

My sister has always been the talented one in the family. Her name is Andrea, though we've never called her that. She has always been Andy to us, and if our parents ever called her Andrea Gayle, we knew she was in big trouble.

I have always been amazed by Andy who seems to be able to do everything and anything that requires creativity. She plays the piano, sings, and draws well enough that at one point in her life, she wanted to be a fashion designer. Ever the artist, she even paints.

Throughout my life, when people would ask me about my talent, I would always defer to my sister and tell them she had all the talent in our family. Being the shy one, I was so intimidated by her outgoing personality, keen sense of humor, and multiple talents that I stayed in the shadows and watched her shine. She was and still is my sun.

As an adult, after I married Michael and stopped working, I considered taking painting lessons. The familiar old tune began playing in my head, reminding me that she had all the talent, but I realized, for the first time in my life, that I didn't *know* if she had all the talent or not; quite simply, I'd never even *tried* to paint. I signed up for art lessons that week.

The teacher provided us with a list of necessary supplies, as well as a guidebook for the class. I was to start the next day. Although I bought the supplies, I had had a busy day, and we had plans that evening, so I had no extra time to read the first three chapters that had been assigned to me.

My class began in early morning, and I went to class as a bundle of nerves. Not only had I convinced myself once again that I had no talent, but I hadn't read any of the instruction book either. I'd never even attempted to draw or paint because I was so fully frozen, trapped by the unfounded belief that I could do neither. A timid type, I was filled with fear that I'd make a fool of myself. I had not a clue how to begin, and class was about to start. As I reprimanded myself for signing up in the first place and for not having read my assignment on top of that, I seriously considered bolting from the whole affair. As I sat wondering whether or not I should exit, that familiar telepathic voice pierced my thoughts, assuring me clearly and unmistakably in the kindest of tones, "I will help you."

It was more than amazing! There I was in an art class, and

my benevolent watcher was right there with me. Guardian angels evidently stand ready and beside us at all times, waiting until they are needed. Perhaps art class seemed a little mundane for support from another realm, but I nodded at the words, as though to a visible source of assurance.

Our first assignment was to draw a pear sitting beside a bowl. Our initial sketch was to be left so the teacher could see how we had used the demonstrations in the book I had not read. I sat there without a clue about where to begin.

Then, I was somehow guided in how to proceed. I began drawing lines this way and that, until I had what was, to me, an amazing pear, with a portion of a bowl for its backdrop. Proud and thankful beyond words, I began to relax. I had evidently drawn what was represented in the first three chapters, as instructed.

My teacher walked among the students and made approving sounds or small critiques. When she arrived at my desk, she made no comment about the perfection I saw in my work; in fact, she seemed irritated. Her emphatic response, in a rather loud tone that could be heard by the class, was, "No, no, no! That work doesn't come until Chapter Four! I told you to work from the first *three* chapters. You have worked ahead of the class!" I guess the first three chapters must have bored my invisible companion.

To this day, I'm not sure if I can draw or not. I never tried again and never went back for more lessons, as writing is my first love. As I try to do with all life experiences, though, I did learn something from that class. I learned that help is available to us at any given moment. We can always receive divine assistance and guidance, even in circumstances that are not life-altering. The unseen world is listening and senses our emotional barometers at all times. Even though I had not verbally asked for help and had not uttered my need in prayer, my hand was guided that day, as surely as the sun comes up in the morning and the moon is there at night.

That was all I needed to know. Learning how to draw had been secondary to the teaching I received that day from the spiritual realm.

## CONNECTION

I'm not even sure how to tell this story, as it's not one I tell often, even though it's one of my most recent experiences.

One day in healing class, while I was watching a demonstration, out of nowhere, my chest began to constrict, as though a huge bandage around my ribcage and chest was being tightened. The intensity of this uncomfortable sensation increased until I could hardly take a breath. I was sure I was having a heart attack. When I felt I could breathe no longer, I reached out my hand to alert the person next to me. Before I made contact, however, I realized that the continued constriction had stopped and was holding its own. A few seconds later, very gradually, the pressure abated, leaving me feeling cold and my chest feeling bruised. That was in November, about two weeks before Thanksgiving. I couldn't quite figure out what had happened, so my daily life resumed after that class quarter adjourned.

In mid-January, my stepdaughter came to visit. She told me about a friend of hers, who had married a very prominent attorney in town. The attorney had died of a heart attack a couple of months before, and her friend was experiencing a lot of problems with the estate. Since I'd worked with attorneys before my marriage to Michael, out of curiosity, I asked his name, only to discover I had dated that attorney for several years before I met Michael. We'd had an extremely close bond, and we continued to be close friends for several years, until our relationship subsided. By the time I met Michael, we had begun to lose touch with each other and had gone our separate ways.

I didn't find out about his death until late January, but he'd evidently had a heart attack the day he returned from guest speaking to a class at Rice University. Curious, I looked up his obituary. The onset of his heart attack had happened about two weeks before his death on Thanksgiving Day. He had lingered in the hospital, hooked up to machines for a while, until he made his transition. Curious, I compared the date of his heart attack with the date I had been away at school, when I had experienced the painful constriction in my chest. Both incidents had happened on the exact same day!

I hadn't seen or talked to the man in over seventeen years. Although I occasionally wondered about him and recalled our relationship, I was very happy that we had not proceeded with more serious plans. I was now happily married, and I realized that the prior relationship would never have worked out. Still, for some reason, that connection evidently lingered, for I somehow experienced part of what he was experiencing during those last days of his life—seventeen years later, with no contact in between.

A few months went by, and thoughts about the incident slipped away. One night, though, in one of the most vivid dreams I've ever experienced, I saw him standing several feet in front of me, slightly elevated above the ground, as though he was on a slanted pathway. I was so happy to see him alive that I began to walk toward him. His arm was extended toward me, with his palm turned upward, his fingers beckoning me forward. A fog was swirling around his lower legs, so I couldn't see his feet. Though no words were spoken between us, his piercing gaze bored into me as he motioned to me again to come with him. Amazed to see him, I continued to move forward to greet him, but then I suddenly stopped. He motioned to me to continue, his eyes looking at me questioningly, but I *knew* I was not meant to touch his extended hand. With his arm still extended toward me, again he motioned more urgently for me to come with him, and when I shook my head from side to side, indicating I could not, he disappeared. Even now, I feel that if I had taken his hand, I would not have awakened that next morning.

## NEW MEXICO

A few years had passed since I had taken solitude and quietude for myself in an attempt to go deeper within in my quest for spiritual connection. I decided to go to Santa Fe for my retreat, since my experiences there had been so extraordinary. I fondly remembered the Chinese herb shop experience, among others. It was just a few fresh years into our marriage, and Michael was very supportive.

I flew to Albuquerque and rented a car to complete the trip to Santa Fe. I had been in the cityscape for several years without a break, so when I drove the vast desert highway between those two cities, I suddenly had the acute sense that I had been living in a box. At that moment in time, the sides of that box were being folded down and away from me, allowing a feeling of great expansion to envelope me.

I realized I had been in the city for so long, with its tall skyscrapers and crowded living conditions that I had been living vertically. Now, I was suddenly engulfed in a large expanse of horizontal space. It was like a giant hug, only in reverse. Instead of being constricted, I was expanded. It was as though my spirit was performing a huge, long-overdue stretch that the city's constricted space didn't allow. At once, I felt welcome.

I drove past Santa Fe to Ojo Caliente, the desert springs that are a sacred spot to some Native Americans. For hundreds of years, perhaps thousands, its waters were used for healing. In the 1500s, the Spaniards stopped there and wrote that the greatest gift the Indian people had was that area and its springs.

I had reserved a cabin, and I couldn't wait for my getaway to begin. *What should I do first? Meditate? Submerge myself in one of the healing spring water baths? Write?* I only had four days, and I wanted to make the best use of every minute.

When I tried to meditate, in spite of my peaceful, natural surroundings, my mind was like a ping-pong ball and refused to settle. The same held true when I attempted to write: I'd pick up the pen and put it back down, pick it up, put it down. I bathed in the waters, but even that didn't help either. I was positively driven from the inside out to use my time to reconnect in the deepest way with the Universal Source. My constant question was: "What should I be doing? How can I create the clearest, closest channel with You?"

I wasted so much time trying to figure out what I should do that I did nothing, and soon, the time for my return was practically upon me. Frustrated beyond words, I finally went outside and climbed up a huge hill that overlooked the compound. When I reached the top, I caught my breath, sat down, and was swept away by the view in all directions. That seemed to calm the compulsive behavior I had been personifying since my arrival.

I decided to meditate in the fresh air and sunshine, atop that rocky mound, and ask the question one more time. After all, I had to leave the very next day. I sat down in relative stillness, closed my eyes, and asked again, "What should I be doing?" Then I remained silent. The answer this time was immediate and loud! That male voice that comes to me from time to time, always sparingly succinct, gave me the answer to my question. After all my searching for the best possible way to reestablish my connection with the unseen Observer , the forceful answer seemed so simple: "Just be!"

I had forgotten that the trick to success in any spiritual endeavor is to send forth a *quiet* intention, keeping a sense of quietude in the mind and in the bodily movements. I had been internally screaming my question, running from this thing to that, keeping my body in motion and my mind always stirring with the need to know instead of allowing it to unfold. One cannot force the desired connection; it is only in *allowing* it rather than trying to make it happen that we get our answers. Remembering to allow was the lesson I took home with me when I left that sacred spot.

**PIXELS**

Michael and I were downtown when he decided to stop by his office as it was nearby. I didn't feel like going into an office building on such a beautiful day, so I chose to wait in the car, since he was only going to be gone for a few minutes.

It was such a glorious day, though, that I felt drawn to get out of the car and wait for him in the fresh air, where a thick carpet of green grass surrounded an adolescent tree. I don't know what drew me out of the car, but it felt like a good idea at the time, so I went with it.

Surrounded by several tall office buildings and lots of concrete, it was nice to be in that small, rare, green space. As I stood by the tree watching for Michael, I reached out and touched the trunk of the tree with my palm. All at once, the world went into a tilt, and I saw all of creation in particles. The buildings weren't solid anymore; rather, they were tiny particles, all separate from one another, divided by air. The best way to describe it is to say that everything I looked at was in pixels, made up of the most vibrant colors. The buildings were still there, but they were shimmering as each molecule danced independently from its neighbor. I had been given a gift, the chance to see that the solid structures of matter as we know them are not solid at all. They exist at all times as vibrating energy, the very basis of the whole Universe, of creation itself. Thus, energy is greater than matter, and as it's always in motion, it can never become stagnant. Jasmuheen writes in her book, *In Resonance,* "Without motion (vibration) there cannot be energy, and without energy there cannot be motion. Thus, molecules are always moving without ceasing, no matter how imperceptibly, and in order for the molecules to move, there must be *space* in between them." Somehow, at that moment in time, the division between each particle of matter became apparent to me as the structures before me shimmered with pure energy.

I had just begun to marvel at the beauty of it all when I heard Michael call to me. As soon as I heard my name, everything transformed back into the appearance of solid form, but although the moment was lost, that memory is still vivid.

## JOEY

One day, when I returned home to the ranch after running errands, I found a small dog tied to a tree, right outside our front door. How odd that seemed. I opened the door and called to my husband. When Michael didn't respond, I assumed someone must have come to visit, and the two of them had gone off together and left the dog safely tied to the tree in our yard until they returned.

When my husband came back, no one was with him, so I asked about the dog. He told me he had found it in our pasture. It was so frightened that it had taken him about thirty minutes of reassurance before it had allowed him to grab the leash it was dragging. He didn't know what to do with it once he had rescued it, so he tied it to the tree to wait and see what I thought when I returned home.

We questioned the residents in the surrounding homes and ranches, hoping to find its owner, to no avail. Odd as it may sound, my soul felt convinced that some kind of spiritual challenge had been placed before me, that it was my assignment to take care of that small, frenzied, lost, confused dog until we could resolve the problem. The only problem was, every time Michael entered the house, the dog went mad, barking nonstop until Michael left the room.

We had a glassed-in sun porch with glass doors between the porch and our living space, so that area became the new dog room; at least with the glass doors closed, the barking was muted considerably. Days went by, and we still could not find the dog's rightful owners.

Finally, our neighbor's wife called me and confided to us that the dog was hers, but she said she couldn't take it back. She shared with us that her husband had once again had too much to drink, and he had tied the dog to a tree and he proceeded to engage in target practice a few feet from where the little canine was tied. Each shot he took went directly over the dog's head, and the gunshots had just about driven the little dog mad. All things considered, she had decided that for her own safety, she needed to leave her husband, and she couldn't take the dog with her. We named the dog Joey, but we knew he couldn't be a permanent part of our family, because he now had a profound fear of men.

One month dragged into three as I tried to find a home for Joey, and Michael's patience was wearing paper-thin. We had words about it more than once, and time was running out for the little guy. Quite frankly, looking back, I'm not really sure how he stood the barking as long as he did.

I decided to make flyers to post in Austin, as the population was much greater there. Plus, our second home was there, so we went back and forth a lot. I posted my heartfelt message in places where I thought the clientele would have a kindness quotient, but no one called, and we were at our wits' end. I wanted to find the absolutely right home for the small dog who feared men, something I felt was my spiritual obligation, and Michael was just trying to live a life of peace and quiet in his own home.

Finally, after we had "the dog discussion" again, he went outside, and I went into our bedroom in tears and fell down on my knees and gave it to God. My heart was heavy and torn, and that plea came from the very depths of my soul. Although I don't remember the exact words, it was something along the lines of, "I can't take this anymore, God, and I don't have the answer. Please help me find the *right* home for Joey. I give it up to You." At the end of that prayer, the phone immediately rang, and that prayer was answered, just that quickly!

A woman in Austin had a friend who wanted a dog. The friend worked long hours and had no other pets, and the lady on the other end of the phone thought a dog would be nice for her friend to come home to at night. She had seen my flyer with Joey's picture on it, and she thought he would be the perfect dog for her friend. She explained, "We have a dog who looks just like him, and we are absolutely in love with him. He's even got his own room, with a queen-sized bed to sleep on." She wanted Joey to make her friend as happy as they were with their own dog.

I had a dilemma to solve, but I didn't want Joey to go to just *any* home to solve my problem. To fulfill what I had come to consider my spiritual test, it had to be the *right* home. I didn't think being alone all day would suit Joey. The woman also worked long hours, and she had no other pets for his companionship in her absence. Nevertheless, the woman on the phone was so in love with her dog that it felt like *her* home was the perfect place for our little canine foundling.

There is no mistaking that Source put that woman's finger to the phone that day in answer to my prayer. Although she protested, I told her I thought her home sounded like the perfect home for Joey, and I suggested that he could be a companion to her other dog. Earlier in our conversation, she had shared that their dog was still grieving over the recent loss of its canine partner. To me, the only deal-breaker, other than her weak protests, would be Joey not bonding well with her husband.

When I took Joey to meet them, the woman and I stood chatting alone in their kitchen. I was holding Joey when her little dog came in to check out the new company. The two dogs could have been twins, as they were the same breed, color, and size.

When her husband came into the kitchen, without saying a word, he walked straight over to me and removed Joey from my arms and snuggled him to his big chest. Joey did not utter one bark, nor did he try to struggle. It was clear that he felt as if he'd come home. He gave out a big sigh as he relaxed into the big man's chest, and he responded as though, after a long journey, his heart had been put to rest. If dogs could smile, that would have been the expression on Joey's face.

Just then, their small nephew ran into the house, and we were introduced. It was even more amazing that the little boy's name was Joey. So, Joey the dog went to live with that family of love, who had a dog who looked just like him and a nephew that shared his name.

How can one even begin to wonder if the Quiet Listener had heard my prayer and brought me the answer I sought? How could one wonder whether or not I saw these "coincidences" as signs that I had successfully completed my test or what I perceived had been asked of me? I choose to believe it was Divine intervention in answer to my pleading prayer that gave the little dog a new, happy life. I also choose to believe there are no coincidences.

Even though they eventually moved to Arkansas, Joey's new family continued to call me once or twice each year to give me updates on his latest antics. After eight years of phone calls, the husband called me one final time in tears to share with me that Joey had stepped over the Rainbow Bridge.

*"Cease trying to work everything out with your minds. It will get you nowhere. Live by intuition and inspiration and let your whole life be revelation."*
*Eileen Caddy*

# CHAPTER 10

## Life After Life

### SIGNS

When we begin to connect with Source on a deeper level, signs begin to appear in our outer lives. A deeper connection brings a growing sense of awareness that didn't exist before. When our awareness grows after we are more deeply involved in our inner life, these signs may begin to appear everywhere. Whether or not we question them, it's important that we know from whence they come.

They can often be interpreted as direction from our Creator, who hears and sees all things, or they can be written off as mere coincidence. Signs may point us in a new direction when we've been in question about a particular problem; they may warn us; they may reassure us that we've made the right decision. If we're watchful, we'll get many answers we might otherwise overlook.

Signs come through various mediums, often in the most mundane things. They may come through words or phrases that are repeated numerous times in various conversations with different people. They may come in the lyrics of a song or in a sequence of numbers that repeatedly shows up in your activities. Even a person you haven't seen in a long while may be a sign or, in casual conversation, something they mention may hold the answer to a question or decision you may have been pondering. Signs come in such a multitude of ways that I cannot possibly begin to describe them all here, and what may be a sign to one person may be totally irrelevant to another. Signs are usually sent for our own individual direction, not to encompass the masses, although those types of signs can also happen, as the Bible readily demonstrates. Our feelings about these so-called coincidences are what will tell us if they are signs or not. We just need to slow down and pay attention to hear their silent language.

The following is an excerpt from a story, "A Sign from the Heavens," shared by a dear friend, Jihan, regarding her belief in signs:

> For me, my Mithi Ma is the love of my life! You see, my dearest, beloved grandmother whom I call my Mithi Ma in Gujarati, meaning "Sweet Grandmother," physically transitioned as she lay in my arms. As I sat in her bed, holding her body after she transitioned, I felt an emptiness I had never experienced before. I was heartbroken.

> The day after the funeral, my cousin and I drove to the cemetery to visit her gravesite and to recite prayers and light incense, as per our faith tradition. Thereafter, we returned to my aunt's home to join the rest of the family members and shared

heartfelt stories about our grandmother.

That evening, I said my goodbyes to my beloved family members and exited into the rainy night. Before I walked down the stairway and onto the driveway, I looked upward and said, "Where are you, my dearest, beloved Mithi Ma? I miss you so much. Please give me a sign to let me know you're all right."

I looked down to take another step, and when I looked up again, I saw something spinning from the heavens, and it fell in front of my right foot. I looked at it, and it was a small, plastic Hallmark card that I had given to my beloved grandmother some five years prior to that night. I looked above and all around me to see who may have thrown it. There was no one in sight. I was the only one outside my aunt's home at that moment. That was when I realized the importance and power of signs.

Paulo Coelho writes a lot about signs in his books, especially in *The Alchemist*. In those pages, Coelho writes:

Each morning brings a hidden blessing; a blessing which is unique to that day, and which cannot be kept or reused. If we do not use this miracle today, it will be lost. This miracle is in the small things of daily life; we must live in the understanding that at every moment there is a way out of each problem, the way of finding that which is missing, the right clue to the decision which must be taken in order to change our entire future. But how to find the courage for this? As I see it, God speaks to us through signs. It is an individual language which requires faith and discipline in order to be fully absorbed.

Signs have also been a huge part of my life, as explained in the experiences to follow.

**MY MOTHER**

During my teen years, my mother and I made a pact with one another. If she died first, she was to give me a sign that she was still in existence, even after her heart stopped beating. She agreed, then turned to me and asked me to do the same. We sealed our agreement with a handshake and a hug, and from time to time, as the years passed we reiterated the agreement to one another.

Years later, in mid-August, she was diagnosed with metastatic lung cancer. By late October, she was gone. When she was finally preparing for her transition from life as we know it, she was no longer able to leave her bed. She was unable to move or speak, but we took turns holding vigil beside her. It saddened me that life was going on around her, wonderful meals, conversation, and sparse laughter, as she lay in her bed. A woman who had been so full of life was being excluded as she remained in the quietude of her room.

My mother was a basketball junkie, and when it came to her

home team, she tried to never to miss a game. As hearing is the last of our senses to go, I was inspired to bring a radio into her room so she could join us in listening to the broadcast of one of those games, even though my father feared it would only sadden her. We gathered at her bedside as a family while the game was being broadcast. At the end of the game, the score was close, and with only a few seconds to spare, my mother's favorite player scored the winning basket. We all began to cheer and tried to act as normal as possible, but we grew quiet as my mother's lips curled into a slight smile, and she raised her hand ever so slightly, pointing her thumb up toward the ceiling. She had heard the game, and she had heard us. What was more amazing was that she had responded with a thumbs-up, showing her support for the home team. We had gathered together with her in a moment of lightness, and that lightness summoned a reaction that transcended her immobility. Days later, she passed, but that was an unforgettable moment.

I learned an important lesson during that basketball game broadcast. When people are gravely ill, we often shut them away in a room, then whisper and tiptoe around them, hoping not to disturb them. Depending upon their personality, including them in things they love can give them great joy, right up until the very end. Even though they may lie still, with their eyes closed, their ears may still be listening.

When my mother passed, we called the authorities to come and remove her body from the house. When they arrived, my father, sister, niece, and I went into the guestroom next to her bedroom and stood in a circle, holding hands and bowing our heads. We didn't turn on the lights, but the room was full of shadows, due to the hour of day. As my mother's body was taken from her room and through the hallway, past the room we were in, I couldn't help but glance up at her one last time. As I did, the overhead light in our room went on, bathing us in an unexpected light. The light switch was on the wall inside the door that I was facing when I raised my head slightly from prayer to catch one last glimpse at the woman who had borne me into life. There was no other switch, and no one had moved, so the light seemed to come on by itself. I felt it was her goodbye to us, and I knew it was the sign she had promised me in that pact so many years before when I was merely a teenager.

Something else occurred during her last days with us. About two weeks before she crossed The Bridge of Life, as we know it, a white dove began to reside in the back yard. My mother loved wildlife and kept her birdfeeders full at all times, so we tried to emulate her. If nothing else, it gave us a reason to go outside for some fresh air during a very difficult time. That white dove held reign over her yard until the day she crossed over. After that, none of us ever saw it again.

It was not until later in the day of her funeral that we realized we had buried our mother on Halloween. Even on that saddest day of all days, we all began to laugh as we discussed it, knowing that with her wicked sense of humor, she would have laughed with us.

**MY FATHER**

My father has been gone for four years now. He came to visit us from out of state for Thanksgiving, and he never saw his home again. He had heard, of course, about the pact I had made with my mother when the light went on after she crossed over, so he and I then made the same pact. After he left his body, he gave me three signs, not just one.

Dad was an absolute jewel, always considerate to a fault, optimistic beyond description, and the wisest of counselors. He was mischievous too. Words cannot describe the bond between my father, my sister, and me. He was a light in the darkness for so many souls that it's hard to express.

He had a heart attack at our ranch two days after Thanksgiving. We rushed him to the country hospital; they, in turn, rushed him to the nearest city hospital in Austin. For four days, he was on a respirator in intensive care, unable to communicate. Then, miraculously, he was back, doing so well that the doctors removed his breathing apparatus. When he was removed from the respirator, he held court with all the nurses and interns, keeping them in stitches of laughter with his great sense of humor. How refreshing that must have been for those who worked in the intensive care unit where trauma was the norm. Within an hour of being released from the shackles of the respirator, he was sitting up, pert, alert, laughing and joking, without even a rasp in his voice. When I told him he was funnier than a Vaudeville act, I questioned him about his incredible exuberance. He just looked at me with a giant smile and said, "Honey, I have a lot to be happy about. I'm alive!"

Shortly after, he was transferred to a regular patient room and told he could go home the next day, but that was his last night to live, and we ultimately lost him to another heart attack before he could be released.

For fifteen hours, Michael and I stood vigil in his room after he was taken off of the respirator. Again, as our hearing is the last of our senses to go, I softly sang the songs we had sung together as I grew up. I am eternally grateful to God for giving us that additional time together between the first and second time he was removed from the respirator, as well as those continuing hours as he lingered with us before letting go.

Without knowing the future, he and I had been afforded the opportunity to discuss his business matters in depth. He even described his safety deposit box key. "It's an odd-shaped key," he said, "with the inscription of B-120 on it."

After Michael and I left the hospital that final time, we decided to drive out to our ranch to check on things and let the wonder of nature soothe our wounded hearts. We had been back to the ranch only one brief time while the respirator was still breathing for him. On that trip, we had straightened the house, as we had departed in such a hurry those few days before when he initially went to the hospital. We had put everything back in order and spent a bit of quiet time there in contemplation and review.

This time, on our way to the ranch, I realized that although I knew what my father's safety deposit key looked like, I couldn't remember where he had told me I could find it! Michael and I discussed this at length during the drive out. I was in shock, and my memory had experienced a hiccup.

When we opened the front door, we were greeted with an unfamiliar humming sound. We followed the sound to the guest bathroom and discovered that the exhaust fan was on. We knew we would have noticed that sound before we left, after straightening the house on our previous trip. We'd had no need to use the exhaust fan in the guestroom, and the *hum* would have been detectable when we were doing our last check, before closing up the house.

Trying to figure it out, both of our eyes fell on the guest bed where my father had slept. Michael had made my father's bed on our last visit, but there, neatly splayed out in a nice, neat circle on top of the smooth bedspread were my father's keys. As we walked over in disbelief, my eyes fell on the one key that had a further space between it on each side than the other keys, making it stand out from all the rest. It was an odd-shaped key with the inscription "B-120" facing up, It was my father's safety deposit box key.

The truly amazing part was that the ring of keys had been in his bag of belongings when we left the hospital! Michael had seen them when he had packed his things, yet somehow they had been transported from my father's hospital bag, which was still in the car, to the bed. Michael and I had walked side by side to the exhaust fan sound first, then to the bed, without being apart at any time.

How did those keys get from the bag that was now in the car to the bed, laid out in such perfect alignment and spacing? Michael had made the bed on our previous visit and would have had to smooth the covers. And how did that exhaust fan not garner our attention just a few feet from my father's bed when we were there before if it had been on? After all, it was loud enough for us to hear when we entered the front door. For us, there could only be one answer to those questions. We came to the conclusion that the exhaust fan had been turned on simply to get our attention and to draw us into the bedroom so the keys could be discovered. In reality, however, it's still a complete mystery.

As soon as my father stopped breathing after he had been transferred from intensive care to his hospital room, then back into the intensive unit, Michael and I decided to e-mail my sister. She lived out of state, and we had kept her apprised of every piece of news, either by phone or by text. As he was due to be released the next day, she had waited, expecting to be with him when he was released from the hospital so we could both share the duties of his care. I prepared to e-mail the sad news.

This took place during the time when I was studying spiritual ministries and Sufism, and there was much to learn about the Arabic language in those teachings. I tried to e-mail the final news to my sister, but I couldn't get the cursor to go to the left side of the margins. It sat on the right margin, blinking at me without response when I hit the cursor. I finally decided to punch any key to see if that would make it scroll to the left. What came up took a minute to register. I don't have any idea what key I had pushed, but what came up on the right margin was the Arabic symbol for God! I stared at it for so long, Michael finally asked me what I was looking at. Without saying a word, I walked over and showed him. When we both got over the shock of the message my father had communicated to us, Michael took my phone to see if he could fix it; somehow, unbeknownst to me, it had been set to the Arabic language. I didn't even know that setting could be changed, so it wasn't something I could have possibly done myself.

In his mortal state, my father knew nothing about Arabic or the symbol for Allah. He and I hadn't discussed in any detail that part of my studies. As Michael and I stood beside his still body in that hospital room that day, we gave thanks that he had remembered our pact. He had given us a second sign that he may not be in his body anymore, but his soul was soaring!

After he left this life behind in early December, I was called by my guidance to go into retreat. I had seen a date in meditation months before, and at that time, it had held no significant meaning for me. It first came to me in mid-August, a January date that kept circulating through my consciousness over the months, with no further clue as to what the mysterious date meant. I decided it would reveal itself in due time.

In December, while we were traveling to my father's home state to deliver his ashes for the funeral, I discussed with Michael the possibility of creating a forty-day retreat period for myself at the ranch. It then struck me what the date represented. Even though the date of January 27 had started coming to me in August, months before my father's visit and subsequent death, I now knew it was when I was to begin my retreat.

Michael was all for it. During the week, he would stay in the city, take care of things, and work, so I could remain at the ranch and enjoy quietude and submersion in my spiritual practices. He would join me each weekend, and when he did, there would be no electronics of any sort allowed, no television, computers, or radios. We would submerse ourselves in reading and nature, painting, puzzles and games, if we chose to play them. When we did play games, it was only those without electronic persuasions, as we wanted to keep the static out of the atmosphere of that sacred environment we had created during my retreat.

It was a great time in our marriage. Without being tethered to the electronic data streaming into our home, we often found ourselves in quiet discussion. We weren't together every day, so we had new adventures to report to each other at the end of each week. We shared stories with one another about ourselves, things we had never shared before and, of course, my father was a constant topic. Talking was allowed on the weekends, though we kept our phone calls to a minimum during the week, so as to keep our power of intention from straying.

Toward the end of my forty days, I received a phone call from my friend Susan. She had no family, but she had just been admitted to the hospital. It was serious, and she needed someone to be with her. Torn about having my retreat cut short, I realized I was being called back into service. I spent part of my last week of seclusion driving in to spend the day with her at the hospital, then driving back to the ranch for solitude that evening. The drive was a little over an hour each way.

Susan was having a difficult time, and the results from her tests didn't paint a very rosy picture for her future. She was told she would have to be on dialysis for the rest of her life or until they could find a suitable kidney donor. I stayed later than usual to give my support that day, and by the time I left the hospital, the sun was already sinking into the night. I knew I wouldn't be able to get back to the ranch before dark.

It was a moonless night, and I chastised myself for not leaving a light on in the house. Out in the country, away from the streetlights and headlights, the darkness can give new meaning to black. When I arrived, I fumbled with the lock on the ranch gate. It was bathed in the blaze of my headlights, but there was nothing to illuminate the walkway and the entry into my dark house after I drove down the drive.

I opened the front door and left the blackness behind, only to be enveloped in a dim, soft glow inside my living room. It barely offered illumination, but it was warm and welcoming, and I perceived it to have a soft rose color. I was confused, and it took me a minute to realize the soft, rose-hued illumination was emanating from an overhead ceiling fan. That fan had six different buttons, none of which were labeled, so I steered clear of it at all times. I had not turned the fan with the lights on and no one else had a key except Michael, who had not been there. Strangely, the globes in the lights of the fan were white, so that didn't clarify why there was a faint rose glow in the room.

I realize now what that retreat did for me: It put me in a quiet place for healing my heart after the loss of my father. I believe it gave my protective father and I some time alone to make the adjustments we needed to make before going on to our different destinations. By the light that guided me into my dark house that evening, I knew he was still taking care of me. I never saw the rose-colored hue in our house again.

My father was always concerned when Michael traveled for work and I spent time at the ranch alone. I suppose any father would think about the safety of his daughter, and I know he shared the same concern for my sister when her husband traveled as well. Although my forty days were nearing their end, and my father had left his body in December, he was still there with me, protecting me and guiding me, sharing himself with me during our period of adjustment. I know, in my heart of hearts, that he didn't want me to enter a dark house alone. I believe that soft, glowing, rose-colored light had been turned on for me, to welcome me home and to reassure me of my father's never-ending presence, his third sign to me to honor our pact.

**SUSAN**

As I already mentioned, my sweet friend Susan was waiting for a new kidney. She continued her dialysis for about seven months. Michael and I had taken an extended vacation and I was nervous about her wellbeing in our absence, as she had no family to give her support or comfort during that challenging time. I called on a regular basis to check on her, and we had many light conversations as she tried to keep a positive attitude.

A few days before our return, she called me and told me of an experience she'd had after retiring the night before. She explained that she was lying in bed, when a bright light began to fill the room; even with her eyes closed, she could easily perceive the intense brightness. At the same time, a warmth she had never felt before enveloped her. When she opened her eyes, she saw that the light was permeating the room, from corner to corner and ceiling to floor. Knowing it didn't originate from outside her home, she somehow sensed that it was meant for her eyes only.

Within that incredible white light were hundreds of tiny colored lights, twinkling on and off, she said, much like those on a Christmas tree, only smaller. Frightened, she confided that she'd closed her eyes tightly and pulled the covers over her head, but even then, she could see the light until she fell asleep. She began weeping as she ended her story. When I inquired about her tears, she told me she was crying because, for the first time in her life, she knew the true meaning of God's grace.

I was eager to return and continue our conversation, and we made it home in a few days. When I called Susan's home, there was no answer. I called her at work the next day, only to discover that no one there had heard from her in a couple of days. I promptly called the authorities and alerted them to check on her, since she was ill and lived alone, and they soon informed us of dreaded news: Susan had joined the light while sleeping.

**MARK**

Before either of my marriages, I dated Mark. He was handsome and had a great personality, and everyone who met him liked him immediately. He was totally unaffected by his good looks, though, and he had a great sense of humor about him.

One thing we shared was a love for horses. Some of ours were bred to ride and others for racing. I was lucky, because Mark worked my horse and his together when we were preparing to race, before we turned them over to a professional jockey for the final ride on race day.

While training one day, he was breaking one of his horses out of the starting gate. The track had just been plowed and groomed. It had rained earlier in the day, so although the soil on top of the track had dried, the soil beneath was still wet and slippery, which created a hazardous situation. When Mark broke out of the gate on a trial workout, his horse slipped and fell, due to the slick dirt buried under the topsoil. As the horse and rider fell down together, the horse rolled over on top of Mark, leaving him limp on the track as the animal scrambled to its feet. I was not there to see it, but I was called and informed that he was unconscious and had been taken by ambulance to a nearby hospital.

I went straight to the emergency room, where they were already treating him for internal bleeding. Hours passed as I waited in an outer room, barred from seeing him before he was transferred to the intensive care unit. I am happy to say he recovered within a few days and was released to go home and rest so he could resume his daily activities.

A year passed. My mother lived 1,200 miles from me, but her dearest friend was a resident of my town. Her friend had a son who was thirty-six years old, and he had just suffered a fatal heart attack while teaching his art class at a nearby university. My mother didn't hesitate to travel to Austin to attend the funeral and comfort her friend, and I was looking forward to seeing her, even under the sad circumstances surrounding her visit. She stayed at her friend's home in town, and since we loved them both, Mark and I invited them to have dinner with us at our home.

Traveling home after work that evening to help Mark with dinner preparations, I passed the scene of an accident. Although the cars had been removed, there were skid marks and glass everywhere, and the street had just been reopened after the incident. I hoped no one had been seriously injured as I picked my way through the flashing lights and shattered glass.

When I drove into my driveway, I noticed that our company had already arrived and just as I opened the car door, my mother rushed from inside the house to my front porch. She had been waiting for me, and the look on her face told me the news wasn't good. The police had just called a short while before to say that Mark had been in an accident and that he'd been taken to the hospital emergency room. I later found out that it was his accident scene I had passed on my way home.

Entering the emergency room parking lot was a surreal experience, something I had done before, not too long ago. It was as if the horse accident a year prior was nothing more than a dress rehearsal for what was to come. I already knew where to park, where to go, which door to open, what questions to ask, and to whom I needed to speak.

This time, though, I wanted to see him. When the nurses refused to allow it, I asked to speak to someone in authority. Eventually, a kind, middle-aged woman joined me and told me it was against the rules. I was incredibly calm and determined when I assured her that I'd been through it all just a year earlier, almost to the day. I told her I would take less than one minute, that I just wanted to see him, and assured her that I would remain calm if they'd only let me go through those doors to where the doctors were working on him. Though I didn't share it with her, the real reason was because, in the deepest depths of my soul, I knew that if I could just look at him once, I would know in that moment whether or not he was meant to remain part of my world.

She studied me quietly for a short time and then, without further questions, agreed to let me go through the restricted doors, but she warned me again that I could only stay for a minute. It took only one second to answer my question, though I spent the full minute allotted to me by his side. He was unconscious, but they had cleaned his wounds, and he looked quite normal, with only a few scratches. That was amazing, considering the collision he'd suffered, but it only took one second for me to know that he was no longer in his body, not even in that unconscious state. I sensed his life force energy and knew immediately it was too low to sustain him. I kept my part of the bargain and left as quietly as I had entered. Days later, Mark was taken off of the respirator, having suffered too much brain trauma to recover. He died at the age of thirty-six, the same age as the recently deceased son of my mother's friend.

Mark's family was from out of town, so the viewing arrangements were left to me. His brother, Jeff, came to town and helped me pick the casket. The plan was to have the viewing in our town, then transfer his body the next day to have the actual funeral service in his hometown, with his family. I worried whether or not I had made the right choices and if what I had arranged would have met with his approval. I did the best I could, but the question still plagued me.

My father had flown into town for the services, so I was grateful to have both of my parents with me while all of it was unfolding. My father drove us home after the viewing. I was in the front of the car with him, and my mother sat in the back seat. It was an eerie night. As we drove to the house Mark and I had shared in the country, there were no streetlights. There was only the blackness, the low, swirling fog over the road, and an occasional peek at the moon as the dark clouds caught all of its light. My father was hunched over the steering wheel, peering into the darkness as he picked his way through the night.

Exhausted and still questioning whether or not I had done as Mark would have wanted, I laid my head against the back of the seat and closed my eyes for just one second. The instant my eyes closed, I heard Mark's voice inside my head. It was crystal clear, quite loud, and incredibly distinct as he told me with a smile in his voice, "You did good."

I thought about that for a long time afterward, for it was my first experience with a voice being telepathically transmitted to me, and it was *his* voice. I couldn't help but wonder if I had imagined it. I wrestled with that question for months. *Did I fall asleep and dream it? Did I imagine it, or did he really communicate with me?*

A few months later, the thought still had not left me, but I realized the answer. Although he was well educated, he still spoke in many of the colloquial terms and phrases he'd learned in the small town in which he grew up. I realized that if my mind had created that assurance to console me and make me feel better about my choices at the viewing, it would have been in proper grammar: *"You did well."* What I heard, however, was the old familiar phrase he'd spoken many times before when he was teaching his small daughter to ride her first pony: "You did good."

A few weeks passed, and the decision had been made to move our horses from our grounds to his family's property. Allowing them an allotted space within the 620 acres of lakefront property they owned, it would be a big relief in my schedule not to be the sole caregiver. They were to be picked up and transported one designated morning before I went to work.

Usually, summoning the horses up in the morning wasn't a problem, as they liked their feed buckets full. On that particular morning, however, I had scheduled to meet with the hauler, who would transport them to their new home. As luck would have it, they were nowhere in sight, and I needed to leave for work shortly. Calling and whistling for them usually broke them into a dead run for the gate, but that chaotic morning, of all mornings, was the exception. The only response I got was dead silence. There was no nickering or whinnying or hooves pounding the ground as I called and whistled over and over again. Perspiration stuck my hair to the back of my neck as exhaustion overtook me. More than ever before the frustration of my aloneness swept through me. Exasperated, I looked at the sky and shouted as loudly as I could: "Will You help me?"

A deep, deep thirst had overcome my efforts. My throat was dry from calling, and my spirits dragged in the dirt behind me as I entered the house. Just a few feet inside the front door was a faucet. One quick glass of water was all it took. When I walked back outside to begin again, perhaps no more than two minutes had passed, if even that long. But there, waiting at the gate, just a few feet away, were all four horses, standing in a relaxed state, as though it was any other morning.

The pasture in front of me was long and wide before it blended into the distant cover of trees. The distance between gate and trees was flat and far, and a good gallop would have been required to cover that ground. Still, there the horses stood, breathing evenly and calmly, as though no exertion had been required at all. It was as though they had materialized out of nowhere during my quick dash inside the house. I had heard nothing, and the pounding of sixteen hooves would surely have garnered my attention, especially since I'd been waiting for them to come. There was no plausible explanation, except that my angry plea to the heavens had been answered. Whether my assistance came from Mark, who seemed to be lingering with me from time to time, or whether it was the Quiet Comforter, I'll never be completely sure. Perhaps it was both.

About a year after his funeral, I felt drawn to go straight home after work one day. Since Mark's death, I'd found all sorts of excuses not to rush home to an empty house. Seldom did I go right home after work, but on that particular day, I felt compelled to do so. I was still living in our country home, on the outskirts of town, so it was a pleasant drive on a beautiful day. I had nothing in particular on my mind and was just living in the moment, happy for the first time in a long while. I was so pleased that I had chosen to go home in the early evening that I turned the radio up louder and I spontaneously rolled down all the windows and let my hair blow as the fresh air rushed in. The wind was too much with my long hair, though, and I eventually rolled up the windows so I could better see to drive. As the windows went up and everything calmed again, Mark's essence completely filled the car; I don't know how else to describe it, but it became so concentrated I wondered if the windows would blow out. He was filling every space that existed within my car, and he was light and happy, seemingly grinning widely, as though he'd just dropped by to say hi. He was invisible, yet he was as present as if he was sitting in the passenger seat beside me, if not more so. I was so taken by surprise that my mind immediately started trying to figure it out; I could only think about the fact that Mark's essence felt fully present. By the time I figured that out, and decided to concentrate solely on his company, his presence began to dissipate, and as suddenly as he had come, he was gone. I know it was his message to me that all was as it should be, that I should be happy without guilt, and that he was still alive and well in his new surroundings.

## MY GURU

In deep meditation one day, I found myself sitting before my Indian teacher, Paramahansa Yogananda, even though he had made his great transition into the hereafter in 1959, long before I had been drawn to his teachings. While sitting with him, I sensed a crowd of other students around me, but I was so mesmerized by him that I didn't look at any of them. I could not take my eyes off of him as he sat in front of us, crossed-leg yogi-style, slightly elevated and stroking the air above something that reminded me of an enormous artichoke. It emanated fantastic, pulsating colors that made our everyday colors pale in comparison. The vibrant hues extended slightly beyond and all around the delineated outline of the object, as would an aura.

My teacher, who appeared more like a movie projection rather than a flesh-and-blood version of himself, moved his hands rhythmically, with his palms loosely cupped, a short distance from the sides and over the top of the pulsating globe. I was so lost in the colors and the rhythm of his movements that I had forgotten I was not alone there. I suddenly recalled that I was not the only one in the audience watching in fascination. To my great surprise, when I turned to acknowledge the one on my right, there was only empty air. I realized then that I was in a state of pure consciousness, not present in the body at all. The others were none other than part of that collective consciousness, but we were together nonetheless, as though we were being taught some great mystical secret.

To this day, I believe such an experience is exactly what happens to us after we transition from this life. I was as real as real could be, as alive as I'd ever been or possibly more so, only I had no body, nor did anybody else, though we were in a group together in vast alertness, continuing our education on another plane of existence with my deceased teacher. That experience changed me, forever solidifying, like words written in stone, my trust that God has a plan for us far beyond this mortal existence.

I've chosen to share these stories as my way of offering assurance that we are so much more than these physical bodies we temporarily use. We are spirit reflections of the Almighty, and when these bodies are gone, the spirit remains.

*"Death is a beautiful transition into a freer life. The limiting clay garment of the body is put aside. The self-centered nature goes with you to learn and grow on the disembodied side of life and then returns here, into a suitable clay garment and suitable circumstances, to learn the lessons we need to learn. Could we but see a bit deeper into life, we would grieve at birth and rejoice at death. If we but knew how short is the Earth life in comparison with the whole, we would be less troubled with the difficulties of one of our days."*
*Peace Pilgrim*

# CHAPTER 11

## Grace through Gratitude

Through living our best life, we are drawn to live a life with heart bowed to our Creator. During our car trips, we occasionally play something we call The Gratitude Game. One of us starts by stating something for which we feel thankful. The other then does the same. We take turns like this, and it can go on, allowing the miles of our journey to melt away as we bask in gratitude. Our ranch is about an hour and fifteen minutes from our house, and we have found enough things to be grateful for to sometimes engulf the entire commute from ranch to home without running out of gratitude.

If you think about it, just being able to sit there and read these words is something to be grateful for. Certainly, I can count gratitude in my heart that you are still reading this book! If you are holding it, you have functioning arms and hands; give double-thanks for that, for there are those who have to live without them. If you can hear sounds outside your window, you can have gratitude for the gift of hearing for some cannot hear. If your children or grandchildren scamper through the house as you're reading, it's a blessing that you have children to love. If you walk to the mailbox to collect your mail, exhibit gratitude that you have legs to carry you there, for some must rely on a wheelchair. Just reading your mail or this book should remind you to be grateful for your eyes and your mind, for some are blind and some cannot read. We can also find gratitude for everyday sustenance no matter how meager it may be, for there are those who have no food at all and would welcome our scraps as a meager meal.

As I've said many times before, everything in life and beyond is vibrating; nothing is solid matter, even if it appears that way. The molecules within every object and being are vibrating at an almost imperceptible speed. Even our words, actions, and feelings carry a certain level of vibration. Our yearning, gratitude, anger, and joy - each carries a vibration that is interpreted by the Universe. We are being watched and acknowledged at all times, not through open eyes but through vibratory resonance. The Universe responds in kind to the messages we send out. If we feel lack, the Universe sends us more of the same. We must learn to choose our thoughts wisely in order to send to Source the correct message through vibration. If you feel abundance, more will be added to your plate. Old song lyrics in *Ain't We Got Fun* boast, "The rich get rich and the poor get poorer." This is a perfect example, yet it doesn't have to be this way. Albert Einstein explained it this way: "Everything is energy and that's all there is to it. Match the energy of the reality you want, and you cannot help but get that reality. It can be no other way. This is not philosophy. This is physics."

When we're suffering through financial difficulties, we may be filled with worry and fear that we will not have enough. What comes to us as a result of that fear is exactly that: not enough! But when we open our hearts and give it up to our Higher Source to handle, we cease to struggle. Through the cessation of struggle, the vibrations we've sent forth in the ethers of the Universe cease to be stirred by fearful thoughts.

An example of this marvelous truth happened during my summer of healing. As I mentioned, I barely had the money to pay the air conditioner repairman, and my worry was that if I did pay him, I would have no money on which to live. Only after I gave up the struggle and trusted and believed that my cares would be taken care of by the Higher Source that exists in all of our lives did it all did work out in my favor. My ex-husband, an angel in disguise, provided the needed funds within a couple of hours, without me even having to ask!

When we put this law into motion - that like attracts like, our positive words, yearning, gratitude, trust, and belief become keys to the great Door of Mystery. When we hold deep trust and belief through a close personal relationship with our Source, we develop the gift of attracting into our lives that which we need.

When we draw our attention to those things we do have, rather than complaining or worrying over those things we don't, blessings abound. Source sends more of the vibration we are emanating, whatever that is. It is a giant loop. If we are sending out the vibration of gratitude, more things come to us for which to be grateful. Through this continuing process, the more our gratitude grows, the more abundance we experience. It's as simple as that, but the vibration of gratitude must resonate deeply within your heart.

While we are enjoying our new stage of abundance, we must never forget to give back. The more we give, the more abundance flows to us, so it's a win-win situation for all. The more abundance we experience, the more we have to share. Abundance spreads like wildfire. By sharing our gifts with those less fortunate than ourselves, we will be doing God's work. When we're doing God's work, the scales tip in our favor in all areas of our lives. Esther and Jerry Hicks explain this principle beautifully in their book, *The Law of Attraction.*

**SHARING MY MESSAGE**

One day in meditation, a clarity of mind I had never experienced before fell over me. If I had to describe it in visual terms, I could only compare it to a deep, still-water pond, completely covered with moss. As the clarity that came to me continued to reveal itself it was as though the moss on the pond began to dissipate, until it had completely disappeared, leaving the water beneath it crystal clear, allowing me to peer straight down into the deepest depths. It felt as though I was looking into the eye of God.

Unveiled in its cleanest, clearest form, my mind received the following transmission. When I jumped up to grab my pen and pad, the clarity remained as my hand struggled to keep up with the speed of the words that poured out without pause, one after another, tumbling out with the force of a gigantic waterfall:

1. I will have infinite patience if you try.
2. I will answer all your questions.
3. I am God Almighty; I have unlimited power.
4. You have unlimited powers to do My Work.
5. You are my Spirit reflections.
6. We will help others, less fortunate than ourselves.
7. We will show others compassion at all times.
8. You shall agree that work for Me comes first.
9. You shall believe that there is life in all things.
10. Most importantly, know that all things are possible through Me.

I saw no reason to share the message above as part of this book, but now you have read it. Why? Because I was prompted and nudged by the Unseen until I bowed to the directive to include it. I have kept it private all these years, for as Bryan Weiss in *Many Lives, Many Masters* said, "People guard this sort of thing for fear that others may think they are weird." In this transcription, my fingers are sometimes faster than my brain, and I am sometimes the last to know what keys my fingers will light upon to form the words that form these sentences to create this book.

I wrote earlier about having learned my lesson about not

sharing the guidance that comes to me, the lesson I learned when our motor home tire blew. I suppose I've still not yet fully learned that lesson. I have kept this message private for all these years, mostly because I don't often share the messages that come to me. I certainly do not want anyone to think that I consider myself some kind of modern-day Moses, bearing commandments for a new age. But as though I am looking at it with new eyes while I type it, I now realize that this message is not addressing *me* as an individual; it refers to "you" as a collective as well. Though Michael and I have lived for years by these guidelines, it is only now that I recognize that these words were meant to be shared with you, or perhaps the time has just now become ripe for that sharing. By sharing this intimate message with you, I'm forced to get over the fear of what others may think of me and realize that I am merely an instrument for delivery.

These transmitted phrases have been instrumental in guiding us in our daily lives. We have taken them to heart and are living what we refer to as our best life so far. The attachment of "so far" to that phrase allows for expansion, so that life can continue to get better and better for both of us. My prayer for you is that your life will also continue to get better and better, just as ours has, through God's never-ending grace.

I thank you for reading this book. I trust if it has fallen into your hands, there must be a reason. In recounting my spiritual experiences, each word written on these pages has polished my own faith and reaffirmed my own deep love for that Heavenly

Presence that guides me through this maze called life. In some way, I feel that this writing is actually my love letter to God.

My ultimate desire through sharing these words with you is that you may find healing and you may find hope, but above all else, I pray that through these shared experiences, you may re-awaken your own deepest faith, should it be sleeping.

Namasté.

### *PEACE BE WITH YOU*

*"May you find your own place to worship God's gift of creation. May it feed you, nurture you, and always carry you to a place of peace, and may you carry its gentle beauty in your heart for all of your days. Such is the power of nature."*
**Michael Blair**

# Knowing:
# A Spiritual Memoir of Healing and Hope
by Ginger Blair

## READER'S GUIDE

Website/Blog: www.gingerblair.com
Facebook: www.facebook.com/gingerblair

# Guide Contents

I.      Pre-reading Activity
II.     Chapters Briefs / Questions for Discussion or
        Journaling
III.    Recommended Reading
IV.     About Ginger Blair

# I. Pre-Reading Activity

*Knowing: A Spiritual Memoir of Healing and Hope* is a book that chronicles the author's ongoing spiritual journey and her spontaneous remission from cancer through prayer and meditation. It explores the challenges and rewards of pursuing a spiritual life in the modern world.

This book shares her personal story of abuse, financial hardship, a deadly prognosis, and other serious life challenges, but all of these roadblocks to living a peaceful life offered up a powerful pathway to consciousness and a relationship with the Divine that ultimately healed her mind, body, and soul.

**ACTIVITY:** Find a quiet, serene, uncluttered space prior to reading the book. If you are new to meditation, simply light a candle, sit in a comfortable position, and listen to the sounds around you. You may do this independently or with a like-minded group of people. For five minutes, pay attention to your breathing and let your thoughts pass through your mind like clouds. If you are struggling emotionally, physically, spiritually, or mentally, envision a shield of healing white light surrounding you. Clear a space in your heart to experience the author's intention with the book:

- To highlight practical ways to achieve wellbeing and balance in the face of difficult life situations.

- To share a unique spiritual journey in order to inspire others to pursue their own spiritual paths.

- To reveal spiritual truths that reinforce the idea that God is a powerful and ever-present force in one's life Who can be depended on.

# II. Questions and Activities for Discussion or

## Journaling

Below are brief chapter descriptions to prompt you to begin exploring your own spiritual journey. Either in a group setting or independently, these questions are designed to spark a discussion or provide the foundation for deep soul journaling.

## Chapter 1: The Deepest Breath

*I have been praying to God, the Great Consoler, since I was a small girl. One night, a deep, powerful breathing filled my bedroom. There was an intense presence that I called into being...and I was scared. I was always very sensitive to other people, animals, and even plants.*

QUESTIONS:
- *Have you ever had a supernatural experience? If so, describe it and explain how it made you feel or how it informed your spiritual life.*

- *How sensitive are you? How often do you feel the energy of others or the energy in nature or places?*

## Chapter 2: Empathic Childhood

*As a child, I never really understood what made me different. My sense of the world did not entirely match the world that others perceived. My heightened senses gave me an inner knowledge that was hard to explain. I experienced early on that the energy all around us is intelligent, powerful, and generous, and I learned about the laws of the universe through my unseen teachers. It was not until later in life I discovered I am what is referred to as an empath.*

*QUESTIONS:*

- *Do you feel what others feel deeply? How does that influence your sense of compassion or service? How has it been challenging?*

- *What is your prayer practice, and how has it changed over the years?*

## Chapter 3: The Return

*But as life unfolded, and the demands of school, work and relationships consumed my thoughts and time, my connection with the Divine began to recede. I knew I had to tune in, once again, to the endless Source of love and support that I treasured as a child. I learned that it's never too late to return to oneself.*

*QUESTIONS:*
- *How do you spend time with the Divine on a daily basis?*

- *How often do you judge yourself for "mistakes" you've made or time you've "wasted"? Are you ready to let go of the past?*

## Chapter 4: My Summer of Bliss

*After receiving my third cancer diagnosis, I decided to retreat to New Mexico for a solitary spiritual retreat. I was frightened, but I was also guided to hone my skills of intuition and healing and to bring about positive change in my life. I wanted to become more authentic in every way possible. I then realized I didn't need to "go away" to do that. The only place I had to go was "within." So I returned from Santa Fe to my* home in Austin to heal. As a result of acting on the guidance I was receiving daily, I experienced a spontaneous healing and was later given a clean bill of health! By the end of summer, I was virtually penniless but the happiest I had ever been. Now, I just needed to allow that guidance to direct me to the perfect source of income. I learned that He is always there with the answer if we don't get in the way.

QUESTIONS:

- *Are you intuitive? When do you rely on your inner guidance to support you and how?*

- *Describe an experience where you trusted that the Universe, God, Source Energy has provided for your needs.*

# Chapter 5: The Soul's Prescription

*A few years earlier, my life was falling apart. How did I get into this situation? How did I allow myself to become a victim of domestic abuse? As I feared for my life, I continued to call on the Source of All Things to give me the strength to follow my heart and leave a dangerous situation. As my heart healed, I found a new way to live... and beautiful love. I found my soul mate. I learned that when you love yourself, love comes to you.*

QUESTIONS:

- *Do you believe in love? How willing are you to open your heart and let love come into your life?*

- *What are some ways to leave a negative situation and begin the healing process?*

# Chapter 6: The Mirror of Meditation

*The proof of the power of uninterrupted devotion was evident in how my life was improving. The power of those blissful, timeless moments of peace where I could lay my heart at the feet of the Beloved became the spiritual anchor I needed. I learned that the most important part of the journey begins with stillness.*

*QUESTIONS:*

- *How often are you still? Do you meditate daily? If not, are you willing to spend just five a minutes a day connecting with your higher self and the divine nature within?*

- *Can you ask for help? Describe an experience when you became still and discovered that small voice within, guiding you to the support you need.*

# Chapter 7: Transforming Beliefs into Wisdom

*I began to explore even more deeply the various faith traditions of the world. What became clear was that all roads lead to Him. One of the most important steps in the journey is to know ourselves, love ourselves and accept ourselves without reservation. Becoming the eternal student makes you the master of your life.*

*QUESTIONS:*

- *Is life a journey or destination? In what ways can we connect with the present moment?*

- *Which spiritual or religious traditions appeal to you and why?*

# Chapter 8: Simple Acts

*Choices are simple acts. The choice to listen to your body, to extend a kind word, to rest for a moment—we have choices in each moment that lay the groundwork for the next experience that defines our reality. The choice to serve others reaffirms a universal truth that lies in the heart of each human being: we are all one. Simple choices in the present moment create a new reality for oneself and for the world.*

*QUESTIONS:*

- *Do you pay attention to your choices? How often do you ask yourself, "Will this choice help or hurt someone, myself included?"*

- *Can you find time to stop and listen to your body? Are you tired, dehydrated, anxious, or tense? What can you do in this moment to improve your condition? Choose to listen to the signals around you and within you to help you make the best choices.*

# Chapter 9: The Unseen World

*It is so easy to only believe with our eyes. We restrict our "knowing" to experiences, places and people in our physical reality. But that's like going to a beautiful castle and only visiting one room. The life of the unseen is rich and vast. It is filled with the power of intuition and the promise of unconditional love and assistance. I learned that we have an eternal partner in Him.*

*QUESTIONS:*

- *Do you believe in the unseen world and the many gifts it provides? Describe a time when you felt the support of unseen forces.*

- *How often do you ask for help? You don't need to go it alone in this world. Write a plea for help to the world of the unseen and clearly state your needs.*

# Chapter 10: Life After Life

*There is no death. We transition from this world to the next and it is up to each of us to provide loving care and support for those facing this important and holy moment. My mother and I vowed to give each other a sign after death—whoever transitioned first. After her death, I received my sign. I learned that the story of your consciousness does not end with physical death. It's only the beginning.*

*QUESTIONS:*

- *Do you believe in life after death? If so, why? If not, why not?*

- *Do you ask for signs? Describe an experience when you believe a sign from a departed loved one came to you.*

# Chapter 11: Grace Through Gratitude

*Life is beautiful. Although I survived cancer, domestic abuse, and financial difficulties and deeply questioned my purpose in life, I always remembered that, for me, gratitude was the surest path to grace. The Source of All Things is ever present, waiting for us to acknowledge Him and simply continue the divine conversation. I learned that the greatest path to grace is through gratitude.*

*QUESTIONS:*

- *Do you maintain a journal, list, vision board, or gratitude jar to express your thanks for the gifts you receive? Describe how to express gratitude.*

- *How has the grace of gratitude changed your own life?*

# III. Recommended Reading

1. *A Return to Love*, Marianne Williamson (Tate Publishing)

2. *Ask and It is Given*, Esther and Jerry Hicks (Hay House)

3. *Autobiography of a Yogi*, Paramahansa Yoganandya (Self-Realization Fellowship)

4. *Creative Visualization*, Shakti Gawain (Bantam)

5. *Eckhart Tolle*, The Power of Now (New World Library)

6. *In Resonance*, Jasmuheen (<u>Lulu.com</u>)

7. *Open Mind Open Heart*, Fr. Thomas Keating (Continuum)

8. *Quantum Healing*, Deepak Chopra (Bantam)

9. *The Alchemist*, Paulo Coelho (HarperCollins)

10. *The Biology of Transcendence*, Joseph Chilton Pearce (Park Street Press)

11. *The Power of Intention*, Wayne Dwyer (Hay House)

12. *The Seat of the Soul*, Gary Zukav (Simon and Schuster)

13. *The Secret Life of Plants*, Peter Thomkins and Christopher Bird (Harper & Row)

14. *Think and Grow Rich*, Napoleon Hill (Tarcher)

15. *You Can Heal Your Life*, Louise Hay (Hay House)

# III. About Ginger Blair

Ginger Blair has been a writer all her life, and speaks about many of her spiritual experiences. She was most recently featured in _The Amazing Faith of Texas,_ which highlighted her experience as a spiritual seeker. After undergoing a spontaneous remission during a deep meditation, she felt compelled to write her first book, _Knowing: A Spiritual Memoir of Healing and Hope,_ to support people with cancer or other catastrophic illnesses, as well as those going through other life-changing, traumatic experiences. The book was written to inspire hope and provide tactical spiritual teaching and support for those facing uncertain futures.

_Knowing_ also details experiences that might help those who have suffered the loss of a relationship and even those individuals who may be healthy and happy but feel the call to go more deeply within.

Ginger is an experienced public speaker who has been featured in newspapers and appeared on numerous radio and television shows. She and her husband Michael split their time between their home in Austin, Texas and their ranch, where they spend time enjoying each other, nature, and their dog, cat, horse, two miniature donkeys, and three llamas.